GAINES AND COLEMAN

REAL ESTATE

math

SIXTH EDITION

what you need to know

LINDA L. CRAWFORD

Dearborn™
Real Estate Education

This publication is designed to provide accurate and authoritative information in regard to the subject matter covered. It is sold with the understanding that the publisher is not engaged in rendering legal, accounting, or other professional service. If legal advice or other expert assistance is required, the services of a competent professional person should be sought.

President: Roy Lipner
Vice-President of Product Development and Publishing: Evan Butterfield
Associate Publisher: Louise Benzer
Senior Development Editor: Anne Huston
Quality Assurance Editor: David Shaw
Typesetting: Ellen Gurak
Creative Director: Lucy Jenkins

Contents

You and This Book   VII

Pretest   XI

Chapter **One**   REVIEW OF BASICS   1

Key Terms   1

Chapter Overview   2

Numbers and Digits   2

Place Value   2

Rounding Numbers   4

Chapter 1 Answer Key   7

Chapter **Two**   FRACTIONS, DECIMALS, AND PERCENTS   9

Key Terms   9

Chapter Overview   10

Key Symbols   10

Arithmetic Operations   10

Fractions   11

Decimals   17

Percent   21

Percent in Word Problems   24

Percent in Multistep Word Problems   26

Chapter 2 Answer Key   28

Chapter **Three**   USING PERCENT IN REAL ESTATE   29

Key Terms   29

Chapter Overview   30

Calculating Basic Percent Problems   30

Multistep Percent Calculations   37

Calculating Graduated Commissions   38

Calculating Net Commission   40

Chapter 3 Answer Key   42

Chapter **Four**   LEGAL DESCRIPTIONS AND AREA PROBLEMS   43

Key Terms   43

Chapter Overview   44

Descriptions of Real Estate   44

Calculating Number of Acres   49

Solving Multistep Square Footage Problems   52

Solving Area and Volume Problems   53

Area Problems Involving Triangles   54

Formulas to Use in Cubic Measure (Volume) Problems   57

Cost Per Unit   57

Multistep Area Problems   58

Chapter 4 Answer Key   60

Chapter **Five**   MORTGAGE MATH   63

Key Terms   63

Chapter Overview   64

Calculating Interest   64

Using Time in the T-Device   65

Mortgage Financial Packages   67

Mortgage Discount Points   71

Debt Ratios   74

Computing Transfer Taxes on Mortgages   75

Computing Monthly Payments   77

Loan-to-Value Ratio   78

Advanced Mortgage Problems   79

Mortgage Amortization   79

Chapter 5 Answer Key   84

Chapter **Six**   REAL ESTATE TAXES   87

Key Terms   87

Chapter Overview   88

Taxable Value   88

City and County Property Taxes   89

Additional Exemptions from Property Taxes   90

Using the T-Device in Property Tax Problems   91

Calculating the Millage Rate for a Community   92

Special Assessments   94

Real Property Transfer Taxes   94

Chapter 6 Answer Key   98

Chapter **Seven**   APPRAISING AND INVESTING CALCULATIONS   99

Key Terms   99

Chapter Overview   100

Cost Approach   100

Sales Comparison Approach   108

Income Capitalization Approach   111

Gross Rent Multiplier (GRM) and Gross Income Multiplier (GIM)   115

Financial and Investment Analysis   117

Multistep Income Tax Problems   118

Percentage Leases and Indexes   119

Types of Income Used in Investment Analysis   121

Investment Analysis for Broker Candidates   122

Predicting Future Return Rates and Economic Ratios   123

Chapter 7 Answer Key   126

Chapter **Eight**   COMPUTATIONS AND CLOSING STATEMENTS   129

Key Terms   129

Chapter Overview   130

Prorating   130

Prorating Property Taxes   135

Prorating Rent   137

Prorating Mortgage Interest   139

Preparing the Composite Closing Statement   141

Five Parts to the Composite Closing Statement   143

Chapter 8 Answer Key   146

POSTTESTS

Posttest One   149

Posttest One Answer Key   151

Posttest Two   153

Posttest Two Answer Key   155

Posttest Three (Broker Candidates)   157

Posttest Three Answer Key   159

Index   161

You and This Book

Virtually every real estate transaction involves numbers; therefore, it follows that everyone in the real estate business should be proficient with numbers. This book will help both prospective and experienced real estate professionals perform numerical calculations with confidence. It will assist in sharpening the use of simple arithmetic in general—and in the field of real estate in particular. The book is especially designed for those who are preparing to take an examination leading to a real estate license.

OUR GOAL FOR YOU

The aim of this book is to help you become more comfortable with arithmetic basics as they are used in the real estate business. Little or no prior knowledge of either the arithmetic or the real estate field is assumed.

GENERAL ORGANIZATION

This book has been carefully arranged to help you gain skill in solving problems involving numbers. An explanation of key terminology is presented at the beginning of each chapter. Each chapter presents "bite-size" concepts in a format that is easy to reference when studying. Throughout each chapter you will encounter one or more *examples* to illustrate each concept. *Practice problems* are provided throughout each chapter to give you an opportunity to "put to work" the concepts presented. The practice problems are numbered sequentially in each chapter. This numbering system enables you to quickly locate the solution to each problem at the end of each chapter.

Every effort has been made to keep the explanations, problems, and solutions relevant, accurate, and success focused. Conscientious students will acquire the necessary skills to feel at ease when confronted with real estate situations involving numerical calculations.

SPECIAL FEATURES OF THIS BOOK

The table of contents and the index provide you with the means to quickly locate the key points covered in this book. A pretest is included to aid you in assessing your level of understanding *before* you launch into the study of the material. The pretest is presented in a multiple-choice format similar to what you will encounter on your licensing examination. At the end of each pretest question is a chapter number in parenthesis that references where an explanation of the concept tested in that particular question can be found. To help you determine how well you have grasped the material after you have studied it, three multiple-choice posttests are included. Solutions to all pretest and posttest questions follow each test. In between are eight chapters that start with an introduction to basic arithmetic concepts, progress through numerical calculations in specific parts of real estate activities, and culminate in the final chapter, which brings together much of what has preceded it.

Sales associate and broker candidates will find the various calculations in this book to be helpful in preparing for the license examination. New in this edition is a special section on investment analysis designed especially for broker candidates (see Chapter 7).

This book is designed to provide you with what you need to know to successfully perform the various calculations that you will encounter on your license exam. If you take the time and effort to work through each type of calculation presented in *Real Estate Math*, you will be confident and prepared to answer the math questions on your exam!

HOW TO USE THIS BOOK WITH SUCCESS

Work your way systematically through this book. Each chapter is designed to build on what has preceded it. Just lightly reading the material over once constitutes neither studying nor learning. Take the time and make the effort; you will learn and remember what you have studied.

A basic arithmetic review is provided in Chapters 1 and 2. If you are a bit rusty when it comes to arithmetic, the Review of the Basics found in Chapter 1 provides a brief yet thorough refresher.

Study the explanations and examples thoroughly before attempting the practice problems. Once you begin to work the practice problems and are completely satisfied with your skill level in a particular subject area, you may choose to move on to the next subject. If for any given problem you cannot arrive at the correct solution as presented in the answer key, refer back to the page where the applicable concept is explained and illustrated.

Throughout this book, you will discover opportunities to express certain elements differently than the author has. For example, just as one-half may be written ½, 0.5, or .5 and have the same meaning, so a formula may be expressed in different ways without changing its meaning or a problem may be approached differently and yet result in the same answer.

Calculators are a great aid in the business and you should know how to use one with ease. Chapter 2 includes keystrokes for basic arithmetic calculations. The author urges you to use a calculator for all of your calculations to become proficient with its use before taking your real estate license examination and embarking on your new real estate career. Although financial calculators are available, only a basic four-function calculator is needed to work these problems.

ABOUT THE AUTHOR

Linda Crawford has been involved in real estate education since the early 1980s. Linda received a master of science from Florida State University and completed extensive postgraduate work in professional testing at the University of Florida. She is the author of *Gaines & Coleman Florida Real Estate Principles, Practices & Law, Florida Real Estate Exam Manual,* and coauthor of *Florida Real Estate*

Broker's Guide. Linda worked as education coordinator for the Florida Division of Real Estate from 1994 through 1996. She has extensive teaching experience. Linda taught real estate pre-license courses for many years at a Florida real estate school. She also taught undergraduate and graduate level real estate and appraisal courses at the University of Florida.

ACKNOWLEDGMENTS

I am grateful to the following professionals who contributed their knowledge and invaluable suggestions to this edition:

- John N. Anderson, Bob Hogue School of Real Estate
- Robert Gordon, Bob Hogue School of Real Estate
- Ron Guiberson, Bob Hogue School of Real Estate
- Sandi M. Kellogg, Central Florida Community College
- Margaret Nagel, Chicago Association of REALTORS®: REALTORS® Real Estate School and Real Estate Education Company
- Joyce Bea Sterling, Northern Kentucky Real Estate School

Linda L. Crawford

Pre Test

The following pretest is intended to help you determine those areas needing the greatest amount of study. Do not turn to the answer key located at the end of this pretest until you have finished the test. Solutions are provided for each test question in the answer key. Each test question is cross-referenced to the chapter where you will find a detailed explanation of the particular calculation. If you score 80 percent or higher, you may want to be selective in using the material in this book. If you score below 80 percent, you probably should study all of the material carefully.

Hint: If you want to test yourself more than once using this pretest, mark your answer choices on a separate sheet of paper.

---

1. You borrow $20,000 at 10 percent simple interest for 2½ years. When you pay the loan and interest at the end of the loan period, how much will you pay the lender? (Note: Interest is cumulative, but not compounded.) (Chapter 5)

   a. $5,000
   b. $20,000
   c. $25,000
   d. $27,000

2. A broker keeps 60 percent of sales commissions and pays the sales associate the other 40 percent. A sales associate sells 50 acres of land at $900 per acre with a gross sale commission of 10 percent of the sale price. What is the broker's commission? (Chapter 3)

   a. $1,800
   b. $2,700
   c. $4,500
   d. $4,700

3. A broker earned a $3,120 commission for selling a residential lot at $52,000. What was the sale commission rate? (Chapter 3)

   a. .06
   b. .08
   c. .60
   d. 16.67

4. At the end of 1½ years, you repay the bank $16,800, which includes $1,800 interest. What was the simple interest rate? (Chapter 5)

   a. .07
   b. .08
   c. .10
   d. .12

5. What is the annual premium for an insurance policy in the amount of $25,000 if the cost is $.60 per $100? (Chapter 3)

   a. $15
   b. $150
   c. $416
   d. $500

6. A developer is subdividing a 12-acre tract into lots measuring 80' × 110'. Each lot has a perimeter of 380 feet and a sale price of $4,500. She has allowed 126,720 square feet for required streets, sidewalks, and recreational facilities. How many salable lots are there? (Chapter 4)

   a. 14.4
   b. 59.4
   c. 45.67
   d. 116.6

7. Mr. Garcia's monthly mortgage payment for principal and interest is $264.60. If his annual property taxes are $780 and his homeowner's insurance premium is $198, what is his total monthly payment, including taxes and insurance? (Chapter 5)

   a. $329.60
   b. $346.10
   c. $379.10
   d. $527.60

8. An investor is considering the purchase of a duplex for $215,500 cash. She wants an investment that will produce a first-year 12 percent net return on investment. How much net income must the duplex generate during the first year to produce this investor's required return on investment? (Chapter 7)

   a. $9,625
   b. $11,550
   c. $12,500
   d. $25,860

9. You have sold a residential property for $98,500. Your employment contract specifies that you receive 55 percent of the total sale commission for properties you sell. If the rate of commission is 8 percent, what amount will you receive? (Chapter 3)

   a. $3,546
   b. $3,940
   c. $4,334
   d. $7,880

10. A buyer has made an earnest money deposit of $7,000 on a home selling for $139,900. A bank has agreed to lend the buyer 80 percent of the sale price. How much additional cash must the buyer furnish to pay the total required down payment? (Chapter 5)

   a. $7,000
   b. $11,920
   c. $20,980
   d. $27,980

11. A bank has agreed to lend $92,000 for 30 years at 7.5 percent interest. The borrower is charged two discount points. If the loan is held for the full term, what is the lender's approximate yield? (Chapter 5)

   a. 7.5 percent
   b. 7.75 percent
   c. 8 percent
   d. 9.5 percent

12. Mr. Jones borrowed $85,000 at 7.5 percent interest per year and paid a total of $3,187.50 in interest. How long was the term of this loan? (Chapter 5)

   a. Two months
   b. Three months
   c. Four months
   d. Six months

13. A seller received $52,000 from the sale of his home. He paid $2,500 in settlement costs in addition to an 8 percent commission. What is the selling price of the home? (Round to the nearest dollar.) (Chapter 3)

   a. $54,500
   b. $56,522
   c. $58,860
   d. $59,239

14. The loan-to-value ratio offered by a local financial institution is 75 percent. If a buyer wishes to acquire a property selling for $129,500, what will her down payment need to be? (Chapter 5)

   a. $1,727
   b. $5,180
   c. $32,375
   d. $97,125

15. Buyers have obtained a mortgage loan of $122,000 at 8½ percent interest. The loan will be amortized by equal monthly payments of $938.07 over 30 years that include principal and interest. How much of the buyers' second month's payment will be applied to the principal? (Chapter 5)

   a. $73.90
   b. $74.43
   c. $148.33
   d. $863.64

16. A property has an assessed value of $125,500. What is the property tax based on a rate of 25 mills? (Chapter 6)

    a. $313.75
    b. $3,125
    c. $3,137.50
    d. $3,150

17. The city is proposing to pave the streets in your neighborhood at a cost of $40 per foot of frontage. The city will absorb 25 percent of the cost. Your lot has footage on the street of 130 feet. Assuming there are homes on both sides of the street, what is the amount of your paving assessment? (Chapter 6)

    a. $1,950
    b. $2,600
    c. $3,900
    d. $5,200

18. Assume the documentary stamp tax on deeds is $.70 per $100 and the total documentary stamp tax charged for a property is $825.30. Calculate the purchase price. (Chapter 6)

    a. $57,750
    b. $82,500
    c. $117,857
    d. $195,835

19. The N½ of the NE¼ of the SW¼ and the S½ of the SE¼ of a section contains how many acres? (Chapter 4)

    a. 2.5
    b. 20
    c. 80
    d. 100

20. You are appraising a three-year-old, single-family residence. The total square footage of livable area is 2,050. The garage is 500 square feet. According to figures obtained from a cost-estimating service, the base construction cost per square foot of livable area is $52 and $36 per square foot for the garage. Calculate the reproduction cost new of the structure. (Chapter 7)

    a. $73,800
    b. $88,600
    c. $106,600
    d. $124,600

21. The net income from a commercial building is $96,000. Assuming a capitalization rate of 11 percent, what is the value of the property (to the nearest dollar)? (Chapter 7)

    a. $105,600
    b. $111,000
    c. $776,727
    d. $872,727

22. An apartment building consists of 10 units that rent for $475 per month each. Vacancy and collection losses are estimated at 4 percent of potential gross income, and management expenses are estimated at 5 percent of effective gross income. Additional miscellaneous operating expenses total $23,700. What is the net operating income? (Chapter 7)

    a. $20,964
    b. $28,170
    c. $28,284
    d. $31,020

23. A buyer purchased a home and is assuming the outstanding mortgage balance of $90,000. The interest rate is 8 percent per year and is due in arrears on the first of every month. The closing is scheduled to commence on July 15. Day of closing is to be charged to the buyer. How much will the seller owe the buyer for accrued interest, using the exact number of days in the month? (Chapter 8)

    a. $276.16
    b. $290.32
    c. $300
    d. $309.60

24. A duplex is scheduled to close on September 10. The seller collected rent for September on the first of the month amounting to $950. According to the sale contract, the buyer is due the rental income for the day of closing. What is the proration? (Chapter 8)

    a. $285 debit to seller, $285 credit to buyer
    b. $633.33 credit to seller, $633.33 debit to buyer
    c. $665 debit to seller, $665 credit to buyer
    d. $665 credit to seller, $665 debit to buyer

25. What is the documentary stamp tax on a deed, based on a rate of $.70 per $100 for a property selling at $123,557? (Chapter 6)

    a. $395.38
    b. $741.60
    c. $864.90
    d. $865.20

PRETEST ANSWER KEY

1. *c.* $25,000

$20,000 loan × 10 percent interest × 2.5 years =
$20,000 × .10 × 2.5 = $5,000 interest + $20,000
principal = $25,000

2. *b.* $2,700

50 acres × $900 per acre = $45,000 total sale
price; $45,000 sale price × .10 commission =
$4,500 total commission; $4,500 × .60 broker's
share = $2,700 broker's commission

3. *a.* .06 or 6 percent

$3,120 commission ÷ $52,000 sale price =
.06 rate or 6 percent

4. *b.* .08 or 8% percent

$16,800 total – $1,800 interest = $15,000 loan;
$15,000 × 1.5 years = $22,500;
$1,800 interest ÷ $22,500 = .08 or 8 percent
simple interest rate

5. *b.* $150

$.60 ÷ $100 = .006 premium rate;
.006 × $25,000 policy = $150 premium

6. *c.* 45

43,560 square feet per acre × 12 acres =
522,720 total square feet – 126,720 square feet for
streets, sidewalks, etc. = 396,000 available square
feet; 80 feet × 110 feet = 8,800 square feet per lot;
396,000 available square feet ÷ 8,800 = 45 lots

7. *b.* $346.10

$780 ÷ 12 months = $65.00 taxes per month; $198
per year ÷ 12 months = $16.50;
$264.60 principal and interest payment +
$65.00 + $16.50 = $346.10

8. *d.* $25,860

.12 net return × $215,500 purchase price =
$25,860 net income

9. *c.* $4,334

$98,500 sale price × .08 commission rate =
$7,880 total commission; $7,880 total
commission × .55 sales associate's share =
$4,334 commission due sales associate

10. *c.* $20,980

$139,900 sale price × .80 = $111,920 loan;
$139,900 sale price – $111,920 loan =
$27,980 down payment;
$27,980 – $7,000 earnest money deposit =
$20,980

11. *b.* 7.75 percent

⅛ × 2 points = ²⁄₈ = ¼; ¼ + 7½ = ¼ + 7²⁄₄ = 7¾ =
7.75 percent approximate yield

12. *d.* Six months

$85,000 loan × .075 interest rate =
$6,375 interest per year; $6,375 interest ÷ 12 months
= $531.25 per month; $3,187.50 ÷ $531.25 =
6 months

13. *d.* $59,239

$52,000 sale proceeds + $2,500 settlement costs =
$54,500; $54,500 ÷ .92 = $59,239.13 or $59,239
sale price

14. *c.* $32,375

$129,500 sale price × .75 LTV = $97,125 loan;
$129,500 sale price – $97,125 loan =
$32,375 down payment

15. *b.* $74.43

$122,000 loan × .085 = $10,370 interest/year;
$10,370 interest ÷ 12 months =
$864.17 interest in month 1;
$938.07 payment – $864.17 interest =
$73.90 principal in month 1;
$122,000 – $73.90 principal =
$121,926.10 outstanding loan balance;
$121,926.10 × .085 = $10,363.72 interest/year;
$10,363.72 ÷ 12 months =
$863.64 interest in month 2;
$938.07 payment – $863.64 interest =
$74.43 principal in month 2

16. *c.* $3,137.50

$125,500 × .025 property tax rate = $3,137.50

17. *a.* $1,950

$40.00 × .75 homeowner's share = $30.00
homeowner's cost per foot of frontage;
$30.00 × 130 feet of footage =
$3,900 ÷ 2 = $1,950

18. *c.* $117,857

$825 documentary tax ÷ ($.70 ÷ $100) =
$825 ÷ .007 = $117,857 purchase price

19. *d.* 100

640 acres ÷ 4 ÷ 2 = 80 acres;
640 acres ÷ 4 ÷ 4 ÷ 2 = 20 acres; 80 + 20 =
100 acres

20. *d.* $124,600

2,050 square feet of livable area × $52 cost per square foot = $106,600;
500 garage area × $36 cost per square foot = $18,000; $106,600 + $18,000 = $124,600

21. *d.* $872,727

$96,000 net income ÷ .11 capitalization rate = $872,727 property value

22. *c.* $28,284

$475 × 10 units × 12 months = $57,000 potential gross income; $57,000 × .04 = $2,280 vacancy and collection loss;
$57,000 − $2,280 = $54,720 effective gross income;
$54,720 × .05 = $2,736 management expense;
$2,736 + $23,700 = $26,436 total expenses;
$54,720 − $26,436 = $28,284 net operating income

23. *a.* $276.16

$90,000 mortgage × .08 interest ÷ 365 = $19.726027 daily interest;
$19.726027 × 14 days = $276.16

24. *c.* $665 debit to seller, $665 credit to buyer

$950 ÷ 30 days = $31.666667/day; $31.666667 × 21 days = $665.00; Seller has collected the rent in advance; Seller owes buyer; Debit seller and credit buyer

25. *d.* $865.20

$123,600 ÷ $100 increment = 1,236 tax increments; 1,236 × $.70 = $865.20

Chapter One

REVIEW OF BASICS

Decimal relating to the number 10; based on 10

Decimal Fraction the digit or digits to the right of a decimal point (.6 or .738)

Decimal Point the period located immediately after the units, placed to show that place values to its right are less than 1

Decimal System a place-value method of using numbers based on 10; each place to the left of the decimal point indicates that a number is raised to a higher power of 10, and each place to the right of a decimal point indicates division by 10

Digit any one of the symbols 0, 1, 2, 3, 4, 5, 6, 7, 8 or 9 used for writing numbers

Mixed Number a number consisting of a whole number and a fraction

Place Value the weight given a digit because of its position in a number

Rounding expressing in approximate numbers rather than exact numbers

Rounding Place in a number, the location of the digit that will determine the degree of accuracy desired

Whole Number a digit from 0 to 9 or a combination of digits located to the left of a decimal point

Chapter | **Overview**

Chapter 1 and most of Chapter 2 review basic arithmetic concepts. If you have any difficulties with arithmetic, or if you need a brush up (and many of us do on occasion!), these chapters will refresh your memory of basic skills and help you to gain confidence. If you have a solid understanding of basic arithmetic, proceed immediately to page 24, Percent in Word Problems.

NUMBERS AND DIGITS

We use numbers every day to communicate with one another. Suppose you are asked to fill the car with gas and pick up a dozen eggs and a half pound of cheese. Not a single number was actually given, but look at the numbers that are directly and indirectly involved. Do you have enough money? How far will you have to drive? How much time will it take? The answers to all of these questions, as well as the quantity and cost of eggs and cheese, involve numbers. There is no need to be uneasy about the use of numbers. You already use them all the time. Numbers are merely symbols to express ideas, and *arithmetic* is a term to indicate a system for the orderly expression of numbers.

The symbols 0, 1, 2, 3, 4, 5, 6, 7, 8, and 9 are **digits.** Digits are used to form *numbers*. A number may consist of only one digit or it may be composed of a great many digits. It is important to remember that the digits 0, 1, 2, 3, 4, 5, 6, 7, 8, and 9 are all available for use. For example, 9 is a number and 9,999,999 is also a number.

Proper order is important in the use of numbers. For example, although the very same digits are used in 1,009 and 9,001, the order (arrangement of digits) causes the latter number to express a far greater value and a very different thought than the former number.

PLACE VALUE

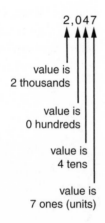

2,047

value is
2 thousands

value is
0 hundreds

value is
4 tens

value is
7 ones (units)

To ensure understanding and uniformity, the location of digits in a number determines their **place value.** Place value is the relative value or weight given a digit because of its position in a number. A **decimal point** is the period located immediately after the units, or ones, place to show that place values to its right are less than 1. The word **decimal** means based on the number 10. Because the system of numbers we use is based on the number 10, it is called the **decimal system.** If no decimal point is written, then a decimal point is implied to the right of a number immediately after the last digit (the units place). A digit's relationship to the decimal point—written or unwritten—determines that digit's place value. For example, the second digit to the left of a decimal point has a place value 10 times greater than the place value of the first digit to the left of the decimal point. The third digit left of the decimal point has a relative value 100 times the place value of the first digit. This concept is shown in the illustration at left.

A value scale (as shown below) has been established for standardizing the place values of the digits used in forming numbers. The farther left of the decimal point a digit is located, the greater its relative value.

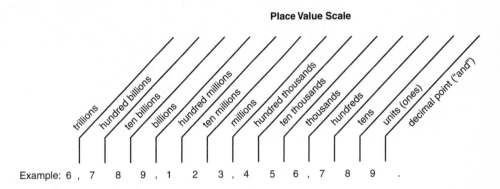

Place Value Scale

Example: 6 , 7 8 9 , 1 2 3 , 4 5 6 , 7 8 9 .

Notice the use of commas in the above whole-number example. Moving from the decimal point to the left, a comma may be inserted between the third and fourth digits, another between the sixth and seventh digits, and so on. When a number has four or more digits, it is much easier to read the number if the digits are separated by commas (for example: 6,789,123,456,789 versus 6789123456789).

Now that you know the place value assigned to each digit (refer to the value scale), write the number 6,789,123,456,789 in words instead of digits.

_____

_____

Did you write six trillion, seven hundred eighty-nine billion, one hundred twenty-three million, four hundred fifty-six thousand, seven hundred eighty-nine? Good for you if you did. You are correct!

Note that the word *and* is not used in writing whole numbers, even long numbers. For example, 934 is not expressed as nine hundred *and* thirty-four. To be correct, say and write nine hundred thirty-four. Do you follow this rule when writing checks?

The word *and* indicates the location of the decimal point and marks the exact location where a whole number ends and a part of a whole number, called a decimal fraction, begins. A **whole number** may be defined as a digit from 0 to 9 or a combination of digits, such as 28 or 17,567. A **decimal fraction** may be defined as a part of a whole unit, such as .4 or .8642. A **mixed number** is a combination of a whole number and a decimal fraction or a common fraction, such as 6.25 or 6¼. A common fraction can express the same numerical value as a decimal fraction but in a different form. Common fractions are explained in the next chapter.

To express an idea more precisely than is permitted by whole numbers, decimal fractions may be used. Decimal fractions extend the capabilities of the whole-number system by indicating fractional parts of a whole unit. Decimal fractions expand the usefulness and accuracy of the place value. It breaks a whole unit down into an almost infinite number of parts.

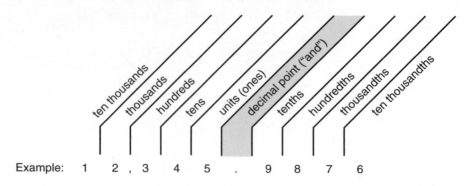

Place Value Scale

12,345.9876

Example: 1   2 , 3   4   5   .   9   8   7   6

The correct way to write the number under the above scale is twelve thousand, three hundred forty-five *and* nine thousand eight hundred seventy-six ten thousandths.

Remember that all digits to the right of a decimal point make up a decimal fraction, and they represent a numerical value less than 1.

> **Hint:** Commas are *not* used to the right of the decimal point, regardless of the length of the decimal number (3,426.36412).

PRACTICE PROBLEMS

Test your understanding of place values. Write each of the following numbers in words:

1. 4,296 _____

2. .0184 _____

3. 758,420 _____

ROUNDING NUMBERS

When we use an approximation for a number, we say that we are **rounding** the number. For example, in some situations, a less precise numerical value could be given; thus the number 72.96821 might be expressed as 73. In other cases, more precision may be required, but perhaps not to the extent of having to use all five decimal places. The **rounding place** digit is the one that indicates the degree of accuracy desired. For example, when rounding the above decimal number to hundredths, the digit 6 (in the hundredths position on the place value scale) is the rounding place digit. Once you decide on the degree of accuracy that is necessary, use the following rules as guidelines for rounding numbers:

Step 1   Find the place to which you wish to round (the rounding place) and look at the digit to the right.

Step 2   If the digit to the right is 5 or greater, add 1 to the marked digit. If the digit to the right is less than 5, leave the marked digit unchanged.

Step 3   When rounding a *whole number*, all digits to the right of the rounding place digit are replaced by zeros.

When rounding a *decimal fraction*, if the marked digit is to the left of the decimal point, replace each digit to the right of the marked place with '0,' and drop all digits to the right of the decimal point. If the marked digit is to the right of the decimal point, drop all digits to the right of the rounding place.

Rounding reduces the accuracy of a number value and replaces it with a more generalized value. "There were 973 people in attendance" is a more accurate count than "There were about 1,000 people in attendance" (rounding to the nearest hundred).

Appraisers in all fields frequently must round off their estimates to the nearest hundred dollars. For example, if an appraiser's computations produce the numeral $46,461, he or she would normally round that number to the nearest hundred dollars, or $46,500. To leave the appraisal at $46,461 would imply a degree of accuracy not often possible.

Example: Round 52,487 to the nearest hundred. _____

Note that you are rounding a whole number to the nearest hundred. Which is the rounding place digit? Counting from the right (units, tens, hundreds), you determine that the digit 4 is the rounding place digit so you increase the 4 to a 5 and substitute zeros for all digits to the right of the rounding place. Thus, rounding 52,487 to the nearest hundred becomes 52,500.

Example: Round 52,487 to the nearest thousand. _____

When rounding 52,487 to the nearest thousand, you find that the digit 2 is in the thousands position in the numeral. Thus, 2 becomes the rounding place digit when rounding to the nearest thousand. Because the number immediately to the right of the rounding place is 4, the rounding place digit remains unchanged. Then substitute zeros for all whole numbers to the right of the rounding place digit 2. Thus, rounding 52,487 to the nearest thousand becomes 52,000.

Example: Round 6.0448 to the nearest tenth. _____

The nearest tenth indicates that the rounding place will be the first digit position to the right of the decimal point. Decimal fraction rules apply. A look at the tenths position on the place value scale reveals that a zero is the rounding place digit in this example, with a 4 on the immediate right. The digit in the rounding place (0) is left unchanged, and the 4 (along with the digits to its right) are dropped.

Some will, no doubt, suggest that both the 0 and the 4 in the above example be dropped. To do so would ignore the degree of accuracy required. The question asked that 6.0448 be rounded to the nearest tenth. Therefore, 6.0 establishes accuracy between 5.95 and 6.04. If 6 is written, it indicates an accuracy somewhere between 5.5 and 6.4, which would be considerably less accurate than 6.0. In real estate, accuracy is not only a requirement but also a moral obligation when dealing with other people's property and money. In addition, answers on real estate examinations are frequently required to be exact.

Write each of the following in words:

4. 4,345 _____

5. .005 _____

6. 6,253.17 _____

7. 2,450,050 _____

8. .0258 _____

Write each of the following in numbers, excluding common fractions:

9. Three thousand four hundred ninety-four and fifty-six hundredths _____

10. Fourteen million one hundred sixty thousand two hundred twenty-one

_____

11. Ninety-eight million thirty-one _____

12. Two thousand four hundred seventy and ten thousandths _____

13. Six tenths _____

Round each of the following numbers as indicated:

14. To the nearest thousandth
42.06948 _____

15. To the nearest tenth
.68743 _____

16. To the nearest hundredth
4.25389 _____

17. To the nearest cent
$16.78392 _____

18. To the nearest hundred dollars
$4,978.68420 _____

Write the name of the place on the value scale represented by the first digit of each number for each of the following:

19. 4,697.32 _____

20. 926,843 _____

21. 10.09 _____

22. 4,222,613 _____

23. .796 _____

Write the name of the place on the value scale represented by the last digit on the right for each of the following:

24. 21.34 _____

25. .9034 _____

26. 6.4 _____

27. .218967 _____

28. .34713 _____

ANSWER KEY

1. Four thousand, two hundred ninety-six
2. One hundred eighty-four ten thousandths
3. Seven hundred fifty-eight thousand, four hundred twenty
4. Four thousand, three hundred forty-five
5. Five thousandths
6. Six thousand, two hundred fifty-three and seventeen hundredths
7. Two million, four hundred fifty thousand, fifty
8. Two hundred fifty-eight ten thousandths
9. 3,494.56
10. 14,160,221
11. 98,000,031
12. 2,470.010
13. .6
14. 42.069
15. .7
16. 4.25
17. $16.78
18. $5,000
19. Thousands
20. Hundred thousands
21. Tens
22. Millions
23. Tenths
24. Hundredths
25. Ten thousandths
26. Tenths
27. Millionths
28. Hundred thousandths

Chapter Two

FRACTIONS, DECIMALS, AND PERCENTS

K E Y   T E R M S

Common Fraction a number made up of a numerator and a denominator separated by a horizontal or diagonal line ($\frac{5}{8}$ or 8/3 or ⅖)

Denominator the part of a fraction that is below the line (signifies the total number of equal parts in the whole unit)

Dividend a number to be divided

Divisor a number by which a dividend is divided

Fraction part of a whole; may be expressed as a common fraction (¼) or as a decimal fraction (.25)

Improper Fraction a number in that the numerator is equal to or greater than the denominator (⅝ or ⅔)

Mixed Number a whole number plus a fraction

Numerator the part of a fraction that is above the line (signifies the number of parts of the whole unit being counted)

Percent per hundred; per hundred parts

Product the result of multiplying numbers together

Proper Fraction a number in which the denominator is greater than (>) the numerator (⅜)

Quotient the result of dividing one number (the dividend) by another number (the divisor)

Chapter | **Overview**

This chapter focuses on the explanation and general use of fractions, decimals, and percents. The chapter concludes with a discussion of how to calculate the percentage of profit and loss in real estate transactions.

KEY SYMBOLS

= equals	× multiply	< is less than	' minutes; feet
+ add	÷ divide	> is greater than	" seconds; inches
– subtract	% percent	° degrees	∟ right angle (90°)

ARITHMETIC OPERATIONS

There are various ways to express each of the four basic arithmetic operations. For each one, all of the symbols and words shown indicate the same operation.

Addition:	4 + 3	4 and 3	4 plus 3	
Subtraction:	4 – 3	4 less 3	4 minus 3	
Multiplication:	4 × 3	4 · 3	4 times 3	4(3)
Division:	4 ÷ 3	3)4	3 into 4	⁴⁄₃

Since completing school, many adults have had little need to work closely with fractions, decimals, and percents. Real estate, however, is a business that demands dealing with these concepts on a daily basis. Real estate sales associates regularly confront property descriptions in which fractions are used (SE¼). They also regularly encounter decimals when referring to property dimensions (208.71 feet). Real estate professionals regularly see (Yes!) sale commissions figured as a percent of the selling price (7%) as well as a percent of the total sale commission earned (40%).

The list of specific applications could go on and on, but it is safe to say that no real estate professional can adequately perform the necessary daily activities unless he or she has a working knowledge of these and other arithmetic basics. This chapter deals with fractions, decimals, and percents in general and assumes little or no recent experience in these areas on the part of the student. The following chapters cover the use of these three numerical representations as they specifically apply to real estate.

FRACTIONS

$$\frac{3}{4} \quad \begin{array}{l} \text{Numerator} \\ \text{Denominator} \end{array}$$

When a whole unit, or number, is divided into equal parts, each of the parts is a **fraction** (and a percent) of the whole unit. For example, if a city block is divided into two equal parts, each part is one-half (½ or 50 percent) of a city block.

When dealing with fractions, the number below the line is called the **denominator.** The denominator always indicates the total number of equal parts in a whole unit. In the above example of the city block, the fraction ½ has as its lower number (denominator) the digit 2. This indicates a total number of 2 equal parts in the entire city block. If the fraction ¼ had been used, the denominator would have indicated that the city block was divided into 4 equal parts.

The number in a fraction that appears above the line dividing the numbers is called the **numerator.** The numerator indicates how many of the equal parts of the whole unit are being counted. For example, in the fraction ¾, the numerator indicates 3 equal parts are being counted and the denominator shows a total of 4 equal parts, so you are talking about all but one equal part of something (all but ¼).

The line separating the numerator from the denominator means division (the top number is divided by the bottom number). If you are dividing a fraction using a calculator, enter the numerator first, then the division key, followed by the denominator.

A **proper fraction** is a part of a whole whose denominator is always greater than its numerator (½, ¼, ⁵⁄₁₇, ²¹⁄₂₂). An **improper fraction** is one whose numerator is equal to or greater than the denominator (⁴⁄₄, ⁶⁄₄, ¹²⁄₃, ³⁶⁄₃₅). The term **common fraction** includes both proper fractions and improper fractions.

Changing Fractions

To change an improper fraction (when necessary) to a whole number or a **mixed number,** divide the numerator by the denominator.

Example:

$$\frac{8}{4} = 2 \qquad \frac{8}{7} = 1\frac{1}{7}$$

PRACTICE PROBLEMS

Change the following improper fractions to mixed numbers.

1. $\frac{9}{8}$ = _____

2. $\frac{20}{5}$ = _____

To change a mixed number to an improper fraction, multiply the whole number by the fraction's denominator, add the numerator, and place that result over the denominator of the mixed number.

Example: $\quad 7\frac{1}{2}$

Step 1 Multiply the whole number by the denominator. $\qquad 7 \times 2 = 14$

Step 2 Add the numerator. $\qquad 14 + 1 = 15$

Step 3 Place the result over the denominator of the mixed number. $\qquad \frac{15}{2}$

Example: $12\frac{3}{4} = \frac{(12 \times 4) + 3}{4} = \frac{51}{4}$

Or

$$(12 \times 4) + 3 = \frac{51}{4}$$

Hint: Parentheses are used in equations (see above equation) to indicate that the enclosed procedure must be done first.

Change the following mixed numbers to improper fractions.

3. $2\frac{1}{7} =$ _____

4. $21\frac{2}{9} =$ _____

Reducing Fractions

To reduce a fraction, divide both the numerator and the denominator by the same largest possible number, that is, the *greatest common factor*.

Example: $\frac{3}{12} = \frac{3 \div 3}{12 \div 3} = \frac{1}{4}$

When the numerator and the denominator cannot again be divided evenly by a common factor, the fraction is in its *simplest form*.

Reduce the following fractions to their simplest forms.

5. $\frac{7}{21} =$ _____

6. $\frac{3}{36} =$ _____

Finding Common Denominators

Whenever denominators are not the same, fractions cannot be added or subtracted until a *common denominator* is found. The lowest number that can be divided evenly by all of the denominators is called the *lowest common denominator*.

First, make certain that all fractions are in their simplest form. Then test for a common denominator by determining if all of the denominators will divide evenly into the largest denominator. For example, find the lowest common denominator for:

$$\frac{3}{4} , \frac{1}{2} , \frac{5}{8}$$

The largest denominator is 8, and the other two denominators (4 and 2) will divide evenly into 8. Thus, 8 becomes the lowest common denominator.

To restate the original fractions in terms of the new common denominator in the above example; first, divide the new common denominator by each original denominator.

$$8 \div 4 = 2$$

$$8 \div 2 = 4$$

$$8 \div 8 = 1$$

Next, multiply each resulting answer (quotient) by the original numerator to obtain the correct new numerator.

2×3 (from ¾) = 6 is the new numerator of the first fraction

4×1 (from ½) = 4 is the new numerator of the second fraction

1×5 (from ⅝) = 5 is the new numerator of the third fraction

Then, combine the new numerators with the common denominator (8).

$$\frac{3}{4} = \frac{6}{8}$$

$$\frac{1}{2} = \frac{4}{8}$$

$$\frac{5}{8} = \frac{5}{8}$$

Now the fractions are restated in terms of the lowest common denominator and are ready to be added or subtracted.

If this first test for finding the lowest common denominator does not work, test for a common denominator by multiplying the two smallest denominators involved. For example, find the lowest common denominator for:

$$\frac{1}{4} , \frac{1}{6} , \frac{1}{3}$$

The two smallest denominators are 4 and 3, and $4 \times 3 = 12$. Will all three denominators divide evenly into 12? Yes! Therefore, 12 becomes the lowest common denominator.

If this second test does not work, try another pair of denominators, as shown in the following example:

$$\frac{1}{4} , \frac{1}{6} , \frac{1}{2}$$

Because the result of multiplying the two smallest denominators (4×2) is 8, which cannot be divided evenly by all denominators, the next largest pair (6 and 2) should be tried. This yields 12 and can be divided evenly by all three denominators.

If all of the above tests fail, multiply all of the denominators as shown in the following example:

$$\frac{3}{4} , \frac{1}{7} , \frac{2}{5}$$

In this problem, 4×5 does not work, 4×7 does not work, and 5×7 does not work in finding a common denominator. Thus, it becomes necessary to multiply all of the denominators ($4 \times 7 \times 5 = 140$). In this case, 140 is the lowest common denominator.

> **Hint:** If any of the fractions have not been reduced to simplest form, the result may not be the lowest common denominator, but it will yield a common denominator that can be reduced.

Solve for the lowest common denominator:

7. $\frac{3}{4}$, $\frac{1}{8}$ = _____

8. $\frac{6}{8}$, $\frac{4}{6}$ = _____

9. $\frac{3}{4}$, $\frac{1}{7}$, $\frac{3}{14}$ = _____

10. $\frac{1}{9}$, $\frac{2}{7}$, $\frac{1}{4}$ = _____

Adding and Subtracting Fractions

To add or subtract fractions, it is first necessary to determine the lowest common denominator. Then, add (or subtract) the new numerators and place the result over the common denominator. It may be necessary to reduce the resulting fraction to its simplest form.

Examples:

Adding fractions—Find the common denominator and add the new numerators together. Place that sum over the common denominator.

$$\frac{1}{2} + \frac{1}{4} =$$

$$\frac{1}{2} = \frac{2}{4} \; ; \frac{1}{4} = \frac{1}{4}$$

$$\frac{2}{4} + \frac{1}{4} = \frac{3}{4} \qquad \text{(called the } sum\text{)}$$

Subtracting fractions—Find the common denominator and subtract the new numerators. Place that sum difference over the common denominator.

$$\frac{1}{3} - \frac{1}{5} =$$

$$\frac{1}{3} = \frac{5}{15} \; ; \frac{1}{5} = \frac{3}{15}$$

$$\frac{5}{15} - \frac{3}{15} = \frac{2}{15} \quad \text{(called the } \textit{difference}\text{)}$$

11. $\frac{2}{7} + \frac{12}{35} =$ _____

12. $\frac{14}{15} - \frac{1}{4} =$ _____

Multiplying Fractions

To multiply fractions, multiply the numerators, then multiply the denominators, place the product of the numerators over the product of the denominators, and reduce the fraction to its simplest form (if necessary).

Example: $\frac{1}{4} \times \frac{5}{6} = \frac{1 \times 5}{4 \times 6} = \frac{5}{24}$ (called the **product**)

PRACTICE PROBLEMS **13.** $\frac{6}{11} \times \frac{3}{7} =$ _____

To multiply a whole number by a fraction, the whole number is treated as the numerator with a denominator of 1.

Example: $3 \times \frac{5}{12} = \frac{3}{1} \times \frac{5}{12} = \frac{3 \times 5}{1 \times 12} = \frac{15}{12} = 1\frac{3}{12} = 1\frac{1}{4}$

Some multiplication problems can be simplified by reducing numbers before multiplying. To reduce in preparation for multiplying, divide one numerator and one denominator by the same number, and then multiply as before. Using the previous Example:

$$3 \times \frac{5}{12} = \frac{3}{1} \times \frac{5}{12}$$

The numerator 3 and the denominator 12 can both be divided by 3.

$$\frac{\overset{1}{3}}{1} \times \frac{5}{\underset{4}{12}} = \frac{1 \times 5}{1 \times 4} = \frac{5}{4} = 1\frac{1}{4}$$

This crossing out of a number is called *canceling.*

The following example shows the value of reducing to simplest form before multiplying.

$$\frac{7}{14} \times \frac{5}{12} \times \frac{3}{5} \times \frac{3}{8} =$$

If you multiply as is without first reducing, the problem progresses as follows:

$$\frac{7 \times 5 \times 3 \times 3}{14 \times 12 \times 5 \times 8} = \frac{315}{6,720}$$

Try expressing this in its simplest form. Yikes! If you reduce first and then multiply, the problem is not nearly so cumbersome. Thank goodness!

$$\frac{\overset{1}{7}}{\underset{2}{14}} \times \frac{\overset{1}{5}}{\underset{4}{12}} \times \frac{\overset{1}{3}}{\underset{1}{5}} \times \frac{3}{8} = \frac{3}{64}$$

PRACTICE PROBLEMS **14.** $13 \times \frac{2}{11} =$ _____

15. $\frac{1}{36} \times \frac{6}{12} \times 9 =$ _____

To multiply a mixed number by a fraction, convert the mixed number to an improper fraction and complete the problem as you would for the multiplication of fractions.

> **Hint:** Canceling cannot be done until mixed numbers are converted into fractions.

Examples:

$$2\frac{5}{8} \times \frac{1}{2} = \frac{21}{8} \times \frac{1}{2} = \frac{21 \times 1}{8 \times 2} \text{ or } 1\frac{5}{16}$$

$$12\frac{1}{3} \times \frac{2}{3} = \frac{37}{3} \times \frac{2}{3} = \frac{74}{9} \text{ or } 8\frac{2}{9}$$

PRACTICE PROBLEMS

16. $4\frac{5}{7} \times \frac{4}{5} =$ _____

17. $2\frac{1}{2} \times \frac{8}{15} \times 5 =$ _____

Dividing Fractions

To divide fractions, invert (turn upside down) the fraction that you are dividing by (the **divisor**) and complete the problem as you would for the multiplication of fractions (see above).

> **Hint:** You cannot cancel out numbers until you are ready to multiply.

Example:

$$\frac{3}{4} \div \frac{1}{2} = \frac{3}{\underset{2}{4}} \times \frac{\overset{1}{2}}{1} = \frac{3 \times 1}{2 \times 1} = \frac{3}{2} = 1\frac{1}{2}$$

The answer is called the **quotient.**

PRACTICE PROBLEMS

18. $\frac{6}{7} \div \frac{2}{5} =$ _____

To divide a whole number by a fraction, invert the fraction that you are dividing by, and complete the problem as you would for the multiplication of whole numbers by fractions (see above).

Example:

$$4 \div \frac{3}{5} = \frac{4}{1} \times \frac{5}{3} = \frac{20}{3} \text{ or } 6\frac{2}{3}$$

PRACTICE PROBLEMS

19. $17 \div \frac{1}{2} =$ _____

To divide a fraction by a whole number, place the whole number over the denominator 1 and complete the problem as above.

Example: $\dfrac{3}{5} \div 4 = \dfrac{3}{5} \div \dfrac{4}{1} = \dfrac{3}{5} \times \dfrac{1}{4} = \dfrac{3}{20}$

PRACTICE PROBLEMS

20. $\dfrac{1}{2} \div 11 =$ _____

To divide a mixed number by a fraction, convert the mixed number to an improper fraction (see above) and complete the problem as you would for the multiplication of fractions.

Examples: $9\dfrac{1}{3} \div \dfrac{4}{5} = \dfrac{\overset{7}{\cancel{28}}}{3} \times \dfrac{5}{\underset{1}{\cancel{4}}} = \dfrac{35}{3}$ or $11\dfrac{2}{3}$

$7\dfrac{1}{2} \div 4 = \dfrac{15}{2} \div \dfrac{4}{1} = \dfrac{15}{2} \times \dfrac{1}{4} = \dfrac{15}{8} = 1\dfrac{7}{8}$

21. $10\dfrac{1}{5} \div \dfrac{2}{5} =$ _____

DECIMALS

This section focuses on numbers in which the decimal point is involved. Decimal points are much easier to work with compared with fractions, because numbers can be easily added, subtracted, multiplied, and divided using a basic four-function calculator. (A four-function calculator adds, subtracts, multiplies, and divides.) A review of the basic concepts of adding, subtracting, multiplying, and dividing decimal numbers is provided in the next four sections of this chapter. Basic calculator keystrokes are also presented.

Adding or Subtracting Decimals

To add or subtract decimals, vertically line up the decimal points under each other and add or subtract as you would with whole numbers.

Examples: Adding decimals: $1.2 + .05 = \begin{array}{r} 1.20 \\ + .05 \\ \hline 1.25 \end{array}$

Subtracting decimals: $1.2 - .05 = \begin{array}{r} 1.20 \\ - .05 \\ \hline 1.15 \end{array}$

Calculator Method	Adding decimals: 1.2 + .05 =	
	Press	**Display**
	1 then . then 2	1.2
	+ (the plus, or addition key)	1.2 (no change)
	. then 0 then 5	0.05
	= (the equal sign key)	1.25 (the answer, or *sum*)

	Subtracting decimals: 1.2 − .05	
	Press	**Display**
	1 then . then 2	1.2
	− (the minus, or subtration key)	1.2 (no change)
	. then 0 then 5	0.05
	= (the equal sign key)	1.15 (the answer, or difference)

PRACTICE PROBLEMS

22. 23.16 + .067 = _____

23. 11.26 − 1.3 = _____

Multiplying Decimals

To multiply decimals, multiply as you would whole numbers, add the total number of decimal places in all numbers being multiplied, and mark off the product from right to left accordingly. Zero(s) may have to be added to the left if there are not enough digits for the number of decimal places.

Example:

$$\begin{array}{r} 2.67 \text{ (2 places)} \\ \times\ \underline{\ 2} \text{ (0 places)} \\ 5.34 \text{ (2 places)} \end{array} \qquad \begin{array}{r} .124 \text{ (3 places)} \\ \times\ \underline{\ .03} \text{ (2 places)} \\ .00372 \text{ (5 places)} \end{array}$$

Calculator Method	2.67 × 2 =	
	Press	**Display**
	2 then . then 6 then 7	2.67
	× (the multiplication key)	2.67 (no change)
	2	2
	= (equal sign key)	5.34

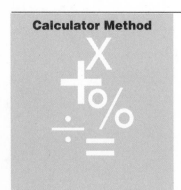

PRACTICE PROBLEMS

24. $27.2 \times 1.11 =$ _____

25. $0.25 \times .04 =$ _____

Dividing Decimals

To divide a decimal number by a whole number, place the decimal point in the answer space directly above the decimal point of the decimal number being divided (the **dividend**) and complete as you would regular division.

Example: $9.03 \div 3 \;=\; 3\overline{)9.03}^{\,3.01}$

Calculator Method

$$9.03 \div 3 =$$

Press	Display
9 then . then 0 then 3	9.03
÷ (the division key)	9.03 (no change)
3	3
= (equal sign key)	3.01

PRACTICE PROBLEMS

26. $18.15 \div 5 =$ _____

To divide a whole number by a decimal, first change the dividing number (divisor) into a whole number by moving the decimal point to the right of the last digit. Write the decimal point after the whole number being divided (the dividend). Then move that decimal point to the right the same number of places as you did with the divisor (the decimal number you started with). Zero(s) will have to be added to the dividend. Next, place the decimal point in the answer space directly above the new location of the decimal point in the dividend. Complete the problem as you would regular division.

Example: $246 \div .2 \;=\; .2\overline{)246}$

$$= \;.2\overline{)246.0} \;\; \text{or} \;\; 2\overline{)2,460}$$
$$= 1,230$$

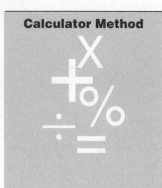

Calculator Method

$$246 \div .2 =$$

Press	Display
2 then 4 then 6	246
÷ (the division key)	246 (no change)
. then 2	0.2
= (equal sign key)	1230

PRACTICE PROBLEMS

27. $3 \div .12 =$ _____

To divide a decimal by a decimal, first change the dividing number (divisor) into a whole number by moving the decimal point to the right. Then relocate the decimal point in the number being divided (the dividend) the same number of places as you did with the divisor. Zero(s) may or may not need to be added. Place the decimal point in the answer space directly above the new location of the decimal point in the dividend, and complete as you would for regular division.

Example:

$$.246 \div .2 = .2\overline{)\,.246\,} = .2\overline{)\,.246\,} = 1.23$$

$$.003 \div .3 = .3\overline{)\,.003\,} = .3\overline{)\,.003\,} = .01$$

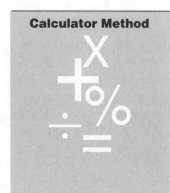

Calculator Method

$$.246 \div .2 =$$

Press	Display
. then 2 then 4 then 6	0.246
÷ (the division key)	0.246 (no change)
. then 2	0.2
= (equal sign key)	1.23

PRACTICE PROBLEMS

28. $.3 \div .12 =$ _____

Changing a Fraction to a Decimal

The line that is located between the two numbers of a fraction means *divided by*. Thus, ½ means 1 divided by 2. The rule for converting a fraction to a decimal is *divide the numerator* (top number) *by the denominator* (bottom number). Or, if you wish, you can express the rule as *divide the denominator into the numerator*.

Example: $\frac{1}{5} = 1 \div 5 = 5\overline{)1.0} = .2$

Calculator Method

$\frac{1}{5} =$

Press	Display
1	1
÷	1 (no change)
5	5
= (the equal key)	0.2

PRACTICE PROBLEMS

Change the following fraction to a decimal.

29. $\frac{3}{8} =$ _____

Changing a Decimal to a Fraction

Knowledge of place value is necessary to convert a decimal into a fraction. With the decimal point removed, the number in question becomes the numerator and the place value of the last digit to the right becomes the denominator. The resulting fraction may or may not be in its simplest form. If it is not, it should be reduced.

Example: $.25 = \frac{25}{100} = \frac{1}{4}$

$.123 = \frac{123}{1,000}$

PRACTICE PROBLEMS

Change the following decimals to fractions.

30. $1.23 =$ _____

31. $.6 =$ _____

PERCENT

Percent means by the hundred or per hundred parts. Thus, when you say 27 percent, you are actually saying 27 parts out of a possible 100 parts. Any percent figure less than 100 percent means a part, or fraction, of the whole. Any percent figure greater than 100 percent means more than a whole unit. For example, 125 percent means one whole (100 parts) plus 25 parts of a second whole. The symbol for percent is %. Any whole (total amount) can be expressed as 100%.

Changing a Percent to a Fraction or a Decimal

In the actual working of a problem involving percent, the percent figure must be changed either to a fraction or a decimal.

To change a percent to a fraction, remember that a percent becomes a fraction when placed over its denominator of 100 (the whole to which it is related). If the percent is a whole number, drop the percent sign, place the number as the numerator over 100, and reduce the resulting fraction, whenever possible.

Examples: $12\% = \frac{12}{100} = \frac{3}{25}$

$150\% = \frac{150}{100} = 1\frac{1}{2}$

Change the following percents to fractions.

PRACTICE PROBLEMS

32. $11\% =$ _____

33. $8\% =$ _____

If the percent is a mixed number:

Example: $7\frac{1}{2}\%$

Step 1 Convert the mixed number to a decimal number.

$$7\frac{1}{2}\% = 7.5\%$$

Step 2 Place the decimal number over the denominator, 100.

$$7.5\% = \frac{7.5}{100}$$

Step 3 Convert the decimal number in the numerator to a whole number by moving the decimal point to the right and adding a zero to the denominator for each place the decimal point in the numerator was moved right.

$$\frac{7.5}{100} = \frac{75}{1,000}$$

Step 4 Reduce the fraction to its simplest form.

$$\frac{75}{1,000} = \frac{3}{40}$$

Example: $8\frac{3}{4} = 8.75\% = \frac{8.75}{100} = \frac{875 \div 125}{10,000 \div 125} = \frac{7}{80}$

PRACTICE PROBLEMS

Change the following percent to a fraction.

34. $10\frac{1}{2}\% =$ _____

To change a percent to a decimal, again remember that the percent sign is dropped and the number becomes a fraction when placed over its denominator of 100.

Instead of reducing the fraction, divide the numerator by 100, which results in a decimal number. Once the above procedure is understood, it is easier to drop the percent sign and just move the decimal point two places to the left, because to divide by 100 means to move the decimal point two places to the left. If necessary, add a zero(s) to create the correct number of places the decimal point must move left.

Examples:

$$40\% = \frac{40}{100} = .40 \text{ (long method)}$$

$$40\% = 40. = .40 \text{ (shortcut)}$$

$$150\% = 150. = 1.50$$

$$7\% = 07. = .07$$

$$7\frac{1}{2}\% = 7.5\% = 07.5 = .075$$

PRACTICE PROBLEMS

Change the following percents to decimals.

35. 24% = _____

36. 1.1% = _____

Changing a Fraction or a Decimal to a Percent

To change a fraction to a percent, first divide the numerator by the denominator. The result is a decimal. Then move the decimal point two places to the right and add the percent sign.

Examples:

$$\frac{1}{4} = .25 = 25\%$$

$$2\frac{3}{4} = 2.75 = 275\%$$

PRACTICE PROBLEMS

Change the following fraction to a percent.

37. $\frac{1}{8}$ = _____

To change a decimal to a percent, move the decimal point two places to the right and add the percent sign.

Examples:

$$3.5 = 3.50 = 350\%$$
$$.007 = .007 = .7\%$$

PRACTICE PROBLEMS

Change the following decimal to a percent.

38. .23 = _____

As a final example of the previous number conversions, examine the following conversion table carefully.

| Percent | Decimal | Fraction | |
		Unreduced	Reduced
100%	1.00	$\frac{100}{100}$	$\frac{1}{1}$
70%	.70	$\frac{70}{100}$	$\frac{7}{10}$
3%	.03	$\frac{3}{100}$	$\frac{3}{100}$

PRACTICE PROBLEMS

Complete the following table:

| | Percent | Decimal | Fraction | |
			Unreduced	Reduced
39.	15%			
40.		.012		
41.			$\frac{625}{10,000}$	
42.				$\frac{1}{20}$

PERCENT IN WORD PROBLEMS

Now that the working relationships between fractions, decimals, and percents have been explained and practiced, it is appropriate to turn to the use of percent as it is found in word problems.

Suppose something costs you $80 and you sell it for $100. What is your dollar profit?

$$\$100 - \$80 = \$20 \text{ profit}$$

What is your percent of profit? The answer to this question is often given incorrectly as 20%. *Profit* is how much you make over and above your cost. It may be expressed as a dollar amount or as a percent of your cost.

The question about percent of profit is asking what part the profit ($20) is of your cost ($80). This relationship can be shown as the fraction $20/$80, which can be converted to a percent.

FORMULA

Percent Profit
Amount made ÷ Amount paid = Percent profit

$$\frac{\$20}{\$80} = .25 = 25\% \text{ profit}$$

To check the answer:

$$
\begin{array}{rl}
\text{cost} = & \$\ 80 \\
\text{profit} = 25\% \times \$80 = & +\ 20 \\
\hline
\text{selling price} = & \$100
\end{array}
$$

If you had answered 20 percent instead of 25 percent, checking your answer would have revealed the following:

$$
\begin{array}{rl}
\text{cost} = & \$80 \\
\text{profit} = 20\% \times \$80 = & +16 \\
\hline
\text{selling price} = & \$96 \quad \text{(An incorrect answer)}
\end{array}
$$

Suppose the problem had stated that something cost you $100 and you sold it for $80. What was your percent of loss? In this instance, you lost $20 of the $100 ($100 – $80 = $20), and you want to know what part this $20 is of the $100. This can be shown as the fraction $20/$100, which can be converted to a percent.

$$\frac{\$20}{\$100} = .20 = 20\% \text{ loss}$$

It is very important that we always determine the correct relationship(s) in any given problem. In the percent profit problem, suppose you had been asked what percent your cost ($80) was of the selling price ($100). You want to know what part the cost is of the selling price. This can be expressed as follows:

$$\frac{\$80}{\$100} = .80 = 80\% \text{ (of the selling price)}$$

Or suppose you had been asked what part (percent) the selling price ($100) was of your cost ($80). Place the selling price over the cost as shown below.

$$\frac{\$100}{\$80} = 1.25 = 125\% \text{ (of the cost)}$$

As you can see, working with these situations involves setting up a relationship in the form of a fraction and then converting the resulting decimal to a percent.

Let's try an example of a real estate related word problem involving percent of profit.

Example: A lot costs $30,000 and sells for $42,000. What is the percentage of profit?

Begin by determining the amount made (profit) on the sale.

$42,000 – $30,000 = $12,000 made on sale

Now it's time to apply our formula:

Amount made ÷ Amount paid = Percent profit

$12,000 ÷ $30,000 = .40 or 40% profit

PRACTICE PROBLEMS

43. A lot costs $40,000 and sells for $48,000. What is the percentage of profit?

Example: A lot sells for $16,000, making a 25 percent profit. What is the cost of the lot?

Uh-oh. What do we do now? Let's see if we can make some sense out of this. We know that whatever the lot cost plus a 25 percent profit equals $16,000. If we accept that 100 percent represents the original cost, we can express this as:

100% cost + 25% profit = $16,000 sale price

or

125% = $16,000

125 percent can also be expressed as 1.25.

1.25 = $16,000

If you recall from high school algebra, we can divide each side of the equal sign by 1.25. 1.25 divided by 1.25 is simply one. The original cost is calculated by dividing $16,000 sale price by 1.25:

$16,000 sale price ÷ 1.25 = $12,800 cost

PRACTICE PROBLEMS

44. A commercial lot sells for $60,000, making a 25 percent profit. What was the cost of the lot?

PERCENT IN MULTISTEP WORD PROBLEMS

What makes a word problem "difficult"? Sometimes word problems require you to demonstrate the ability to perform more than one type of calculation. Often times, a number must first be converted, for example from feet to yards, before you can perform the primary arithmetic operation. Other times you must first calculate a figure (number) before you can insert the number into a formula.

These types of word problems require careful reading to be certain that you are solving for the quantity asked for.

Example: A developer purchases three lots each 100 feet by 125 feet at $300 per front foot. The developer subdivides the lots into five lots and sells them for $22,500 each. What is the developer's percentage of profit on the sale of the lots?

Frontage is often used as a unit of cost in real estate, particularly in commercial real estate. When a lot's dimensions are given, the frontage is always stated first. Therefore, we know that the lots each have 100 feet of frontage.

Step 1 Begin by calculating what the developer paid for the three lots:

$300 per front foot × 100 feet × 3 lots =
$90,000 amount paid for the 3 lots

Step 2 How much did the developer make on the sale?

$22,500 × 5 lots = $112,500 total sale price
total sale price − cost = amount made on sale
$112,500 − $90,000 = $22,500 made on sale

Step 3 Calculate the profit.

Amount made ÷ Amount paid = % profit, so
$22,500 ÷ $90,000 = .25 or 25% profit

PRACTICE PROBLEMS

45. An investor purchases two 100-foot tracts of land for $15,000 per tract. The investor divides the tracts into three equal lots and sells them for $180 per front foot. What is the investor's percent profit?

ANSWER KEY

1. $1\frac{1}{8}$
2. 4
3. $\frac{15}{7}$
4. $\frac{191}{9}$
5. $\frac{1}{3}$
6. $\frac{1}{12}$
7. 8
8. 24
9. 28
10. 252
11. $\frac{22}{35}$
12. $\frac{41}{60}$
13. $\frac{18}{77}$
14. $2\frac{4}{11}$
15. $\frac{1}{8}$
16. $3\frac{27}{35}$
17. $6\frac{2}{3}$
18. $2\frac{1}{7}$
19. 34
20. $\frac{1}{22}$
21. $25\frac{1}{2}$
22. 23.227
23. 9.96
24. 30.192
25. .010

26. 3.63
27. 25
28. 2.5
29. .375
30. $1\frac{23}{100}$
31. $\frac{3}{5}$
32. $\frac{11}{100}$
33. $\frac{2}{25}$
34. $\frac{21}{200}$
35. .24
36. .011
37. 12.5%
38. 23%
39. .15; $\frac{15}{100}$; $\frac{3}{20}$
40. 1.2%; $\frac{12}{1,000}$; $\frac{3}{250}$
41. $6\frac{1}{4}$% or 6.25%; .0625; $\frac{1}{16}$
42. 5%; .05; $\frac{5}{100}$
43. $48,000 – $40,000 =
    $8,000 made on sale;
    $8,000 ÷ $40,000 paid = .20 or 20% profit
44. 100% + 25% = $60,000; $60,000 ÷ 1.25 =
    $48,000
45. $15,000 × 2 tracts of land =
    $30,000 total amount paid for the tracts;
    200 front feet × $180 per front foot =
    $36,000 sale price;
    $6,000 made ÷ $30,000 paid = .20 or 20% profit

Chapter Three

USING PERCENT IN REAL ESTATE

KEY TERMS

Percent per hundred; per hundred parts

Percentage relating to percent; an amount

Base (total) the total amount involved in a problem

Rate a percent of the total; a fractional part of the base (total)

Result (part) the actual amount obtained by multiplying the base by the rate

Chapter | **Overview**

In the real estate business, it is important to develop the ability to solve percent and percentage problems. This chapter helps you build those skills.

In many real estate problems, you may first have to convert fractions to decimals or percents or vice versa. It is easier to work a problem, and you run less chance of making errors, if you express numbers in a consistent form.

To change any percent into an equivalent decimal, simply place a decimal point two places to the left of the number and drop the percent sign.

$$25\% = .25$$

To convert a decimal number to a percent, simply move the decimal point two places to the right and add the percent sign (%).

$$.75 = 75\%$$

To convert a fraction to a decimal form, simply divide the numerator (top number) by the denominator (bottom number).

$$\frac{1}{2} = 1 \div 2 = .50$$

CALCULATING BASIC PERCENT PROBLEMS

In the near future, hopefully you will have the opportunity to calculate lots of earned commissions! But first let's get some commission calculation basics down pat for your upcoming license exam.

To calculate a basic sale commission, take the purchase price times the percent of commission to find the amount of commission.

Example: A property is sold for $96,000. The total sale commission is 7 percent and is divided as follows: the listing office and the selling office will each receive ½ of the sale commission. The sales associate for the selling office receives 60 percent of the selling office's commission. How much does the sales associate earn?

$$\$96,000 \times .07 = \$6,720 \text{ total commission}$$
$$\text{Selling office's commission} = .50 \times \$6,720 = \$3,360$$
$$\text{Selling office's sales associate's commission} = .60 \times \$3,360 = \$2,016$$

This example points to the fact that percents, decimals, and fractions are all related. For example, 6%, .06, and 6/100 are all equal; they are different ways of expressing the same amount.

Percent and Percentage

Some people have difficulty distinguishing percents from percentages. The two are not the same, although both use hundreds as their source.

Percent is technically (and accurately) the **rate**, that is, the fractional part of something. For example, the rate of taxation on a gallon of gasoline may be 9 percent. Rate is expressed as a percent.

Percentage is the actual amount (called a **result**) obtained by applying the above-mentioned percent to a **base** figure, that is, the total amount. For example, assume a rate of taxation on gas of 9 percent. Gas is selling for $1.10 per gallon, and you buy 10 gallons. The percentage is the amount derived:

$1.10 (base price of gas) × 10 gallons = $11.00 (total base cost of gas)
$11.00 × .09 (tax percent) = $.99 (percentage)
(the *result* of multiplying total *base* cost times *rate*)

While closely related to each other, it is apparent that percent and percentage are different things. Their relationship may be described as follows:

- Percent is a rate, so express percent as *rate* (.09 or 9%).
- Percentage is an amount, which is the *result* of multiplying *base times rate* ($.99).
- Base is the total amount involved in a problem ($11.00).

Therefore, the formulas are:

Rate (percent) = Result ÷ Base

Result (percentage) = Base × Rate

Base (total amount) = Result ÷ Rate

A memory device in the form of a common geometric figure is a useful aid for remembering how to solve almost any problem dealing with percents and percentages.

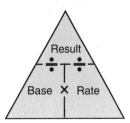

Because the geometric shape can be omitted without losing any of the value of the memory aid, from now on this valuable device will simply be presented as an enlarged letter *T* with the appropriate math symbols included.

Use of the Memory Device

No one learns to play a piano or throw a football without practice. The same is true of arithmetic. Working the practice problems found throughout this book develops your skill and confidence. Practice with various uses of the T-device helps you gain proficiency.

Recall that all percent problems involve three elements (variables). Interest problems involve *time* as well. But the three variables common to all percent problems are:

Rate (percent)

Base (total amount)

Result (percentage, a part of the total amount)

The elements necessary to solve percentage problems are included in the T-device, thereby assisting you to remember and use the three formulas shown earlier. To find the correct operation to solve a problem involving percent or percentage, refer to your memory aid. Note that the horizontal line serves the same purpose as the horizontal line in a fraction—to indicate division.

At least two variables will be given to you in every percent problem, however, sometimes they may not be readily apparent. Careful analysis may be necessary to identify the variables. Once the variables are identified, place them in their appropriate position in the T-device. The missing variable, plus the operation that must be performed, will become apparent.

First, sketch an enlarged letter *T* about the size of the one shown opposite.

Next, place the three mathematical signs in their proper locations as shown.

Finally, assign the three variables to their proper places around the T.

The number on top of the T is always divided by a bottom number. Because the base represents the total amount of something, the base usually will be the largest number among the variables.

> **Hint:** When dividing two numbers using a calculator, enter the top number into the calculator first, next press the division key, followed by the bottom number.

If the rate is the missing (unknown) variable, place your thumb or finger over the place reserved for *rate*. The visible portion of the memory aid that remains indicates that you must divide the percentage result by the base. If it is the percentage result that is to be determined, cover the area of the T reserved for *result;* the operation to perform is Base × Rate. Do not hesitate to sketch this little memory aid whenever solving percent problems.

> **Hint:** If the terms *result, base,* and *rate* seem somewhat foreign to you, consider labeling the parts of your T as follows:
>
> Result (part of the total amount) label simply as *part*
> Rate
> Base (total amount) label simply as *total*
>
> $$\underline{\quad} \div \frac{\text{Part}}{\text{Total} \times \text{Rate}} \div \underline{\quad}$$

Using the T-device to guide us, we have three simple formulas to use for solving percentage problems.

$$\text{Part} \div \text{Total} = \text{Rate}$$

$$\text{Part} \div \text{Rate} = \text{Total}$$

$$\text{Total} \times \text{Rate} = \text{Part}$$

Example: Your customer wants to buy a home selling for $88,000. The best financing available requires a 15 percent down payment. How much is required as a down payment?

What is the *total* amount (base)? $88,000 sale price

What is the percent (*rate*) required 15%
for the down payment?

Solve for the down payment result (*part*). ?

We have been given the *total* and the *rate*. The T-device indicates that we should multiply the total by the rate.

Multiply $88,000 times 15%.
Note that to multiply, you must first
change the 15% to its decimal form (.15).

$$\underline{\quad} \div \frac{?}{\$88,000 \; \times \; 15\%} \div \underline{\quad}$$

$88,000 (total) × .15 (rate) = $13,200 (part) down payment.

Example: Ms. R. U. Shure received a notice from her mortgagee (lender) that last year her total interest paid on a $58,000 mortgage with annual mortgage payments was $3,190. Ms. Shure would like to verify that she is not paying more interest than the mortgage agreement specifies. What interest rate is she paying?

Begin by identifying the parts of the T-device. The $58,000 mortgage is the *total*. The $3,190 payment is the *part*. Solve for the *rate*.

Part $ 3,190
Divided by total $58,000
Equals rate (percent)   ?

$$\underline{\quad} \div \frac{\$3,190}{\$58,000 \; \times \; ?} \div \underline{\quad}$$

The memory device indicates $3,190 ÷ $58,000 = .055 or 5½% interest rate

Example: Mr. Lotsa Dough wants to invest in rental property. You do some investigating and find a property that nets approximately $24,000 annually with an asking price of $187,000. Mr. Dough informs you that he requires at least a 14 percent first year annual return on his money. Therefore, the $24,000 net income must be at least 14 percent of the sale price. Will you advise Mr. Dough to acquire the property in question? Begin by determining which of the variables you have to insert in the T-device:

Part (percentage) $24,000
Rate (percent)   14%
Total   ?

$$\underline{\quad} \div \frac{\$24,000}{? \; \times \; 14\%} \div \underline{\quad}$$

The $187,000 is the asking price, *not* the amount Mr. Dough will pay to get a 14 percent return. Therefore, the *total* is the unknown quantity. The T-device indicates that:

$$\text{Part} \div \text{Rate} = \text{Total}$$

$$\$24,000 \div .14 = \$171,428.57$$

Thus, the most that Mr. Dough should be advised to pay for the property is approximately $171,400.

This same memory device can be used to find assessed value, given a property tax bill and the millage rate. The T-device can also be used to solve for the amount of earned sale commission, given the commission rate and sale price. A little experimentation will reveal an ever-expanding number of situations in which the memory aid can be used.

Example: 61,500 is 93 percent of what number? You should realize that 61,500 is the percentage (*part*) of some larger number, and the percent, or *rate*, is 93 percent.

Using the T-device, the operation indicated is:

61,500 (part) ÷ .93 (rate) = 66,129.032 or
66,129 (rounded) (total)

$$\frac{\$61,500}{? \quad \times \quad 93\%}$$

Example: You paid a 15 percent down payment on a tract of undeveloped land. The down payment amounted to $8,250. What was the purchase price?

Part	$8,250
Rate	15%
Total	?

$$\frac{\$8,250}{? \quad \times \quad 15\%}$$

$$\$8,250 \div .15 = \$55,000$$

It is quite possible to encounter a real estate situation in which a property owner has the information needed to establish a selling price but does not know how to apply the information.

Example: You are negotiating to list a lakefront property. The owner tells you that five of her neighbors have sold their properties within the past six months, and that the five sales reveal that, on average, a property's original cost was 34 percent less than its current selling price. She says she paid $84,800 seven years ago.

With this information, you know that $84,800 is 34 percent less than some unknown *total* amount (property value). Notice that the problem states 34 percent *less than*, not 34 percent *of* some unknown total amount. Therefore, 34 percent is *not* the rate (we cannot simply insert the 34 percent in the T-device).

Because the whole of something is always 100%, the *part* ($84,800) can be represented by 100 percent minus 34 percent or 66 percent. Thus, $84,800 is 66 percent of some unknown amount. Using our T-device we can insert $84,800 as the *part* and .66 as the *rate*.

Part $84,800

Rate .66

Total ?

$$\frac{\$84,800}{? \times 66\%}$$

$84,800 ÷ .66 = $128,484.85 or $128,485 (rounded)

The previous example clearly illustrates that while enough numbers may be given in a problem, they may not be ready to be inserted into the memory aid (or formula).

PRACTICE PROBLEMS

Use the T-device to solve the following problems.

1. Your competitor sold a house for $89,800. The seller said that he paid a sale commission of $4,041. What sale commission rate did your competitor charge?

   _____

2. A client is considering the purchase of a commercial property for $1,522,500 cash. She will not buy unless a reasonable probability exists that the property will produce a 16 percent first year net return on investment. How much net income must the property produce in the first year to qualify for purchase?

   _____

3. The net income of a rental property is $18,000 and the overall capitalization rate is 12 percent. What is the value of the property? (Note: capitalization rates are explained in Chapter 7 in the Income Capitalization Approach section.)

   _____

4. What is the principal balance if the interest amount is $400 for six months at an annual rate of 4 percent?

   _____

Five Steps in Percent Problems

Five steps provide a road map for solving problems involving percent.

Step 1   Read the problem carefully and analyze the situation to determine which variable is missing.

Step 2   Reread the problem statement and label the available information as *rate* (percent), *total* (base), or *part* (result). Simple drawings and arithmetic may need to be done before the labeling can be accomplished. This was illustrated earlier where the original property cost was 34 percent less than the current selling price. You had to find what percent of current market value was represented by a previous purchase price. The previous purchase price was 100 percent less 34 percent, or 66 percent of today's value.

Step 3 Once all of the available information has been labeled, place each variable in the proper position within the T-device.

Step 4 To solve the problem, find the missing variable by performing the arithmetic indicated by the two known variables.

Step 5 Check your answer. Substitute your answer in its proper place as one of the known variables, and pretend one of the other variables is the unknown.

This same procedure may be used for solving all percent problems, regardless of how long or involved they may be. You will find the use of the T-device helpful when calculating sale commissions, depreciation, profit and loss rates, return on investment, tax problems based on percent of purchase price or appraised value, and interest problems—in fact, in all situations involving percent.

Undoubtedly, you will find that you will not need the T-device to help you in analyzing and solving all word problems. The important point to remember is that the T-device is a visual representation of an equation. The number placed on the top of the T (*part*) must be a result derived from multiplication of the two bottom section numbers (the *total* and *rate*).

Sometimes the information provided in a word problem is so abundant that you have difficulty identifying the data needed. Practice is the key. Sometimes the information provided will not be in a form that fits neatly into the T-device. In those situations the information must be converted into a form that can be used. Sketching pictures will help you.

Example: An owner received a net of $67,200 from the sale of his home. The selling broker received a 7½ percent sale commission. What was the total sale price of the home?

It should not take you long to identify the missing variable—the total (sale price) is missing. But when you try to use the information you placed in the T-device, you discover that $67,200 cannot be the correct result if 7½ percent is correct as the rate. The total would have to be an unbelievable $896,000 if both numbers were correct! You know that $67,200 is the *net* amount the seller actually received. You also know that 7½ percent was the commission rate. Aha! The 7½ percent relates to the commission, *not* to the net amount! You have to find the sale price (*total*). If 7½ percent of the total sale price was paid as a commission, then the $67,200 is what was left of the total sale price, or 92½ percent (100% − 7½%). Placing 92½ percent in the *rate* section of the T-device and then performing the arithmetic operation indicated, the sale price (*total*) is found to be:

$67,200 (part) ÷ .925 (rate) = $72,648.648 (total) or $72,650 (rounded)

Use the T-device to solve the following problems.

5. What is 18 percent of $29,000?

_____

6. 6,474 is what percent of 41,500?

_____

7. 291 is 3 percent of what amount?

_____

8. An apartment complex produces a 16 percent return on investment, which amounts to $22,000, in the first year. What did the owner pay for the property?

_____

9. A house sold for $79,000. If the sales associate received $2,765 as a commission for selling the house, what percent of the sale price was her commission?

_____

10. The purchase price on a property was $110,000. The brokerage firm selling the property received one-half of the total commission of 8 percent. How much did the selling firm receive?

_____

MULTISTEP PERCENT CALCULATIONS

Sometimes a math calculation involving a percent requires multiple steps to reach the final answer. You can take comfort in the fact that most of the math questions that you will be asked to calculate will require basic procedures. However, you may encounter one or more advanced word problems. Let's take a look at an example and develop a strategy for tackling similar word problems.

Example: Jack borrows $20,000 at 8% interest. When the loan is paid in full, Jack has paid $800 in interest. How long did Jack borrow the funds?

Step 1 We have three numbers to consider. We know that Jack borrowed $20,000 and that the annual rate of interest is 8 percent. Jack has paid $800 interest. Note that the $800 is _not_ the part because it is not 12 months of interest. The loan amount and the interest rate, however, do belong together so we can use them as the _rate_ and the _total_.

$20,000 (total) × .08 (rate) =
$1,600 simple interest over a 12 month period

Step 2 We know the amount of interest Jack has paid and we know that if he had borrowed the money for 12 months Jack would have owed $1,600 in interest. The $800 is the _part_ and the $1,600 is the _total_. If we plug these into the calculation we will find the rate.

$800 (part) ÷ $1,600 (total) = .50 rate

Step 3 Remember that .50 is equivalent to ½. Jack borrowed the funds for ½ of a year or six months.

11. Devora borrows $30,000 at 6 percent interest. When the loan is paid in full, Devora has paid $1,350 in interest. How long did Devora borrow the funds?

_____

12. Bill borrows 80 percent of the value of a property at an annual interest rate of 6 percent. The first monthly payment of $423.49 includes $400 of interest. What is the value of the property?

_____

13. The monthly interest is $70 on a 6 percent loan. What is the loan amount?

_____

14. Interest paid quarterly is $875. The loan amount is $70,000. What is the interest rate?

_____

CALCULATING GRADUATED COMMISSIONS

Many brokers use various production plateaus as the criteria for increasing their sales associates' commissions. For instance, a sales associate may be paid 50 percent of the broker's commission up to a total production plateau of $200,000 of property sold by the sales associate. From $200,001 to $350,000, the sales associate's share may be increased to 55 percent of the broker's commission, and so forth.

Suppose the broker's listing agreement specified that a 7 percent sale commission was to be paid on the sale price of a parcel. Then assume that a sales associate who had passed the $200,000 plateau sold a property listed by the sales associate's broker. The sales associate received 55 percent of the 7 percent sale commission. Disregarding listing commissions and multiple-listing service (MLS) fees, how much did the sales associate earn if she sold the property for $84,000?

Do you see the similarity between the previous paragraphs and the T-device practice problems after rereading the stated conditions and properly identifying the information provided in the problem?

Step 1 Find the total sale commission:

Rate	7%
Total	$84,000
Part	?

$$\frac{?}{\$84,000 \times 7\%}$$

$84,000 sale price (total) × .07 (rate) =
$5,880 (part—total sale commission)

Step 2 Find the sales associate's commission:

Rate	55%
Total	$5,880
Part	?

$$\frac{?}{\$5,800 \times 55\%}$$

$5,880 total commission (total) × .55 (rate) = $3,234
(part—sales associate's commission)

Once you are confident of the correct procedure to follow, you may no longer need to use the T-device. However, do not hesitate to rely on it when in the process of analyzing a word problem or to use it to assist in labeling the information provided.

At times a broker who lists a property with higher-than-normal value will agree to a graduated sales commission. This provides an incentive for the broker to get the seller the very best price possible.

Example: A broker lists a relatively new office building for sale. He agrees to accept a sale commission of 5 percent on the first $200,000 of the actual sale price, 7½ percent on the next $500,000, 8½ percent on the next $500,000, and 10 percent on anything greater (over $1,200,000). What would the broker's total sale commission amount to if he sold the office building for $2,200,000?

The solving of this problem is best shown through a step-by-step procedure, as follows:

Step 1 $200,000 = first increment of sale price
$\times$ .05 = first increment of commission
$ 10,000 = total first increment commission

Step 2 $500,000 = second increment of sale price
$\times$ .075 = second increment of commission
$ 37,500 = total second increment

Step 3 $500,000 = third increment of sale price
$\times$ .085 = third increment of commission
$ 42,500 = total third increment commission

Step 4 $200,000 = first increment of sale price
500,000 = second increment of sale price
+ 500,000 = third increment of sale price
$1,200,000 = total of first three increments

Step 5 $2,200,000 = total sale price
−1,200,000 = total of first three increments
$1,000,000 = amount to which 10% sale commission is applied

Step 6 $1,000,000 = last increment of sale price
$\times$ .10 = last increment of commission
$ 100,000 = total last increment commission

Step 7 $ 10,000 = first increment commission
37,500 = second increment commission
42,500 = third increment commission
+ 100,000 = last increment commission
$190,000 = total sale commission!!!

Suppose the sales associate who actually negotiated the transaction had been promised 63 percent of the total sale commission. How much would be earned?

$190,000 = total sale commission
$\times$ .63 = sales associate's portion of commission
$119,700 = amount earned by sales associate!!!

15. A building is sold for $160,000. The broker agreed to accept a commission of 7½ percent on the first $100,000 of the purchase price and a smaller percent on anything over $100,000. If the total sale commission is $11,100, what is the smaller rate of commission the broker has also agreed to accept?

_____

16. Cooperating brokers share a 7 percent commission. One broker is due ⅔ of the commission on 30 acres that sold for $2,250 per acre. What is the broker's commission?

_____

17. You have sold a small warehouse for $97,500. Your employment contract specifies that you receive 50 percent of the total sale commission for properties you sell. If the rate of commission is 10 percent, what amount will you receive?

_____

18. The office where you work charges a 7 percent sale commission and pays the listing sales associates 14 percent of the total sale commission on all in-house residential listings sold. The remainder of the sale commission is equally divided between the broker and the sales associate who makes the sale. If you list and sell a property for $75,500, what amount do you receive?

_____

Calculate the missing element for each of the five sales.

	Selling Price	**Commission Rate**	**Commission Earned**
19.	$169,000	_____	$8,450
20.	$80,750	7½%	_____
21.	_____	6%	$5,340
22.	$77,779	7%	_____
23.	$98,000	_____	$7,595

CALCULATING NET COMMISSION

How would you solve a commission problem that asked for the net amount received by the seller?

Example: The sale price is $250,000 and the commission rate is 7 percent. How much did the seller net?

We know that the commission is based on the sale price. However, 7 percent is _not_ the rate. The rate is the percent that the seller receives. Because we know that the whole of anything is represented by 100 percent we can represent the seller's rate as:

$$100\% - 7\% = 93\% \ (rate)$$

The total is the sale price because the seller receives 93 percent of the total sale price. Using our T-device we calculate:

The *total* is the sale price because the seller receives 93 percent of the total sale price. Using our T-device we calculate:

$250,000 (total) × .93 (rate) = $232,500 (part—net to seller)

Now let's consider another example. In this situation we are interested in the sale price knowing what the seller will net, however, there is an existing mortgage on the property.

Example: The seller wants to net $120,000. There is an existing mortgage of $80,000. The broker wants a 7 percent commission. Calculate the sale price.

The commission is based on the total sale price. Total sale price consists of the amount the seller will receive at closing plus the pay off of the existing mortgage.

Seller's net + Mortgage amount = Total sale price

$120,000 net to seller + $80,000 mortgage = $200,000 (part)

Again, we cannot simply use 7 percent as our rate. This is because our *total* is based on the seller's net. Therefore remembering that 100 percent represents the whole of anything:

100% – 7% = 93% rate

$200,000 (part) ÷ .93 (rate) = $215,053.76 (total—sale price)

PRACTICE PROBLEMS

24. The sale price is $145,000 and the commission rate is 6½ percent. How much did the seller net?

_____

25. The seller wants to net $70,000. There is an existing mortgage of $20,000 and the broker wants to earn 6 percent commission. What is the required sale price?

_____

26. The seller wants to clear $110,000. Seller closing costs are $2,000. The broker charges a 6 percent commission. What must the property sell for?

_____

27. The sellers want to net $80,000 from the sale of a property that they own free and clear. The broker wants 7 percent commission and seller closing costs are estimated to be 4 percent. What must the home sell for?

_____

28. The seller wants to clear $100,000. Seller closing costs are estimated at $3,000. The broker charges a 5 percent commission. What must the property sell for?

_____

ANSWER KEY

1. $4,041 commission (*part*) ÷ $89,800 (*total*) sale price = .045 or 4½% (*rate*)

2. $1,522,500 purchase price (*total*) × .16 net return (*rate*) = $243,600 (*part*)

3. $18,000 NOI (*part*) ÷ .12 (*rate*) = $150,000 (*total*)

4. $400 is only six months' interest. The 4 percent is an *annual* rate. Therefore, $400 × 2 = $800 (*part*) interest for 12 months; $800 (*part*) ÷ .04 (*rate*) = $20,000 principal (*total*)

5. $29,000 (*total*) × .18 (*rate*) = $5,220 (*part*)

6. 6,474 (*part*) ÷ 41,500 (*total*) = .156 or 15.6% (*rate*)

7. 291 (*part*) ÷ .03 (*rate*) = 9,700 (*total*)

8. $22,000 (*part*) ÷ .16 return (*rate*) = $137,500 purchase price (*total*)

9. $2,765 commission (*part*) ÷ $79,000 sale price (*total*) = .035 or 3.5% (*rate*)

10. $110,000 purchase price (*total*) × .04 (*rate*) = $4,400 selling office's commission (*part*)

11. $30,000 (*total*) × .06 (*rate*) = $1,800 (*part*) interest for 12 months;
$1,350 (*part*) ÷ $1,800 (*total*) = .75 or ¾ of a year = 9 months

12. $400 single month's interest × 12 months = $4,800 interest for 12 months;
4,800 interest (*part*) ÷ .06 (*rate*) = $80,000 loan amount;
$80,000 loan (*part*) ÷ .80 (*rate*) = $100,000 value (*total*)

13. $70 single month's interest × 12 months = $840 interest for 12 months;
$840 (*part*) ÷ .06 (*rate*) = $14,000 loan amount (*total*)

14. $875 × 4 quarters = $3,500 interest for 12 months; $3,500 (*part*) ÷ $70,000 (*total*) = .05 or 5% (*rate*)

15. $100,000 increment × .075 = $7,500 commission; $11,100 total commission − $7,500 = $3,600 remaining commission;
$160,000 sale price − $100,000 = $60,000 increment;
$3,600 commission ÷ $60,000 = .06 or 6%

16. 30 acres × $2,250 per acre = $67,500 sale price (*total*);
$67,500 (*total*) × .07 (*rate*) = $4,725 total commission (*part*);
⅔ = 2 ÷ 3 = .6666667; so
$4,725 (*total*) × .6666667 (*rate*) = $3,150 (*part*)

17. $97,500 sale price × .10 commission = $9,750 total commission;
$9,750 × .50 = $4,875

18. $75,500 sale price × .07 commission rate = $5,285 total commission;
$5,285 × .14 = $739.90 listing commission;
$5,285 − $739.90 = $4,545.10 remaining commission; $4,545.10 × .50 = $2,272.55 sale commission split;
$2,272.55 + $739.90 = $3,012.45 total sales associate's commission

19. $8,450 ÷ $169,000 = .05 or 5% commission rate

20. $80,750 × .075 = $6,056.25 sale commission

21. $5,340 ÷ .06 = $89,000 sale price

22. $77,779 × .07 = $5,444.53 sale commission

23. $7,595 ÷ $98,000 = .0775 or 7.75% commission rate

24. 100% − 6.5% = 93.5%;
$145,000 (*total*) × .935 (*rate*) = $135,575 net to seller (*part*)

25. 100% − 6% = 94% (*rate*);
$70,000 + $20,000 = $90,000 (*part*);
$90,000 (*part*) ÷ .94 (*rate*) = $95,744.68 (*total*)

26. 100% − 6% = 94% (*rate*);
$110,000 + $2,000 = $112,000 (*part*);
$112,000 (*part*) ÷ .94 (*rate*) = $119,148.93 (*total*)

27. 4% + 7% = 11%;
100% − 11% = 89% (*rate*);
$80,000 (*part*) ÷ .89 (*rate*) = $89,887.64 (*total*)

28. $100,000 + $3,000 = $103,000 (*part*);
100% − 5% = 95% (*rate*);
$103,000 ÷ .95 = $108,421.05 (*total*)

LEGAL DESCRIPTIONS AND AREA PROBLEMS

K E Y   T E R M S

Area the amount of surface contained within a described boundary, stated in square units, such as square feet

Base that side of a geometric figure on which the figure should rest

Height the perpendicular distance from the base of a geometric figure to the highest point

Lot and Block a method of legal description that identifies lots within a recorded subdivision plat map

Metes and Bounds a method of legal description used to describe regular and irregular shaped parcels

Government Survey Method a method of legal description based on a grid system of base lines and meridians

Perimeter the lines forming the outside boundaries of a figure—perimeter equals the sum of all the sides

Per Front Foot The number of feet of frontage of a parcel

Point of Beginning (POB) the starting reference point in the metes-and-bounds legal description

Volume the amount of space within a confined three-dimensional object (cubic measure)

| **Overview**

This chapter focuses on the math calculations associated with legal descriptions. Calculations involving square footage and acreage based on lot dimensions are also explained.

A chart of key measurements follows. Many of these measurements must be used in math calculations. To prepare for your license exam, these measurements should be memorized.

Linear Measure

    12 inches = 1 foot
    3 feet = 1 yard
    5,280 feet = 1 mile

Area Measure

    1 foot × 1 foot = 1 square foot
    43,560 square feet = 1 acre
    1 mile × 1 mile = 1 square mile = 640 acres
    1 section = 640 acres
    36 sections (6 miles × 6 miles) = 1 township (1 T, or 1 TWP)

Volume Measure

    Volume is measured in cubic units. (Check whether your state
      tests volume.)
    3 feet × 3 feet × 3 feet = 27 cubic feet = 1 cubic yard

Directional Notation

    There are 360 degrees (360°) in a circle.
    A circle can be divided into 4 quadrants of 90° each.
    There are 60 minutes (60') in each degree.
    There are 60 seconds (60") in each minute.

DESCRIPTIONS OF REAL ESTATE

The three basic methods of describing real estate—lot and block, metes and bounds, and the government survey system (also know as rectangular survey system)—are explained in the following sections.

Lot and Block

The **lot and block** method of legal description can be used only where plat maps have been recorded in the public records. The platted subdivision is divided into large areas called *blocks,* and each block is subdivided into smaller areas called *lots.* A plat of a subdivision consists of the lot and block identification, the name of the subdivision, and the county in which the subdivision is located. A reference to a particular lot and block in a certain subdivision and county qualifies as a legal description. There is little arithmetic that needs to be done by a real estate professional with this method.

Metes and Bounds

The **metes-and-bounds** method is used to describe both regular and irregular shaped parcels. It is the most accurate method of legal description. The metes-and-bounds method describes land by specifying the boundaries of a parcel. This is done with compass directions, markers (*monuments*) to identify each corner of the parcel, and measurements indicating the length of each boundary. The method is so named because metes refers to *distance* and bounds refers to *direction*.

In plotting metes-and-bounds legal descriptions, the **point of beginning (POB)** and all turning points should be regarded as the exact center of a circle. Always mentally place the POB at the center of a circle and proceed out in a designated direction.

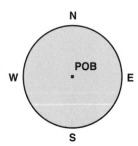

Every compass and every circle has four major directions:

north

south

east

west

If you draw a straight line connecting north and south, you have identified and connected the two primary direction indicators for plotting metes-and-bounds legal descriptions. The first movement from the center of a circle will always be outward in either a north or a south direction.

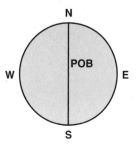 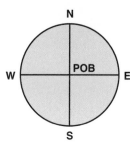

To identify the two secondary direction indicators, draw a straight line connecting east and west. The result is a circle divided into four quarters, or quadrants. Because a circle has 360 degrees, each quadrant measures 90 degrees.

In metes-and-bounds legal descriptions, all directions begin with a reference to either north or south—the primary indicators—and then a rotation (expressed in degrees) toward either east or west, the secondary direction indicator. A distance notation follows the secondary indicator:

Example: **North 30°**   **East 150 feet**

	↑	↑		↑	↑
	primary direction indicator	degrees indicator		secondary direction indicator	distance measurement

The above direction indicators specify the following:

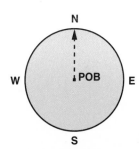

1. Extend a line from the point of beginning at the center of an imaginary circle north to the edge of the imaginary circle.

2. At the edge of the circle, proceed in the direction of the secondary direction indicator (east) the number of degrees stated—30°. Place a mark on the edge of the circle at the approximate place of the specified degree location.

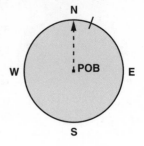

3. Draw a straight line from the center of the circle (POB) extending through the degree location and beyond. This indicates the tract boundary direction.

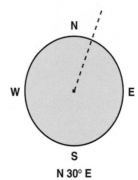

N 30° E

4. Use a scaled ruler such as 1 inch = 100 feet to indicate the distance of 150 feet. The boundary should be extended when drawn to scale.

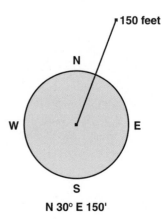

N 30° E 150'

Example: From the brass marker at the center of the intersection of Keyes Avenue and Century Street, proceed North 45°10'30" West 39.80' to the point of beginning. From POB proceed South 89°30'00" West 208.71', thence North 0° 30'00" West 208.71', thence North 89°30'00" East 208.71', thence directly to POB.

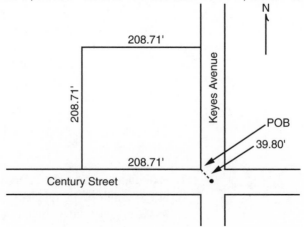

1. Draw a line in the circle to show the direction of a boundary line running South 45 degrees East.

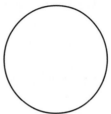

2. Beginning at the southeast corner of a parcel, proceed North 90° West 200 feet to a marker, then proceed North 0° 200 feet to a marker, then proceed South 90° E 200 feet to a marker and then to the original POB. What is the square footage in this parcel?

Rectangular Survey System

The **government survey system** of legal description consists of a grid system of numbered squares, as shown. The primary units of measurement in this system are:

■ **Township**—a square, 6 miles on each side (36 square miles), which can be divided into 36 sections.

■ **Section**—a square, 1 mile on each side (1 square mile). The 36 sections in each township are all numbered and identified in the sequence below.

Township 1 South, Range 1 West

36	31					36	31
1	6	5	4	3	2	1	6
	7	8	9	10	11	12	
	18	17	16	15	14	13	
	19	20	21	22	23	24	
	30	29	28	27	26	25	
36	31	32	33	34	35	36	31
1	6					1	6

1 mi.

N

1 mi.

6 mi.

6 mi.

Each section contains 640 acres and is commonly subdivided into halves, quarters and smaller tracts.

To subdivide a section into quarters:

1. Through the center of a section, draw a vertical line from top to bottom (north to south).

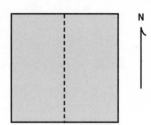

2. Again through the center, draw a horizontal line (west to east).

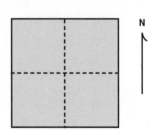

3. The section is now divided into four quarters. The upper right corner of the section is the northeast quarter, the lower right corner is the southeast quarter, and so on, as shown.

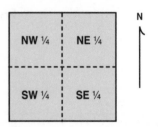

Each quarter section contains 160 acres. To locate a smaller tract, subdivide a quarter section by drawing vertical and/or horizontal lines until you have reduced the area to the size of the desired tract.

To locate property from a legal description, always begin at the end of the description and work back from right to left.

Example: Locate the southeast ¼ of the northwest ¼ of Section 24.

Section 24

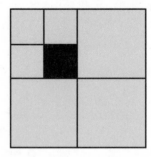

First, locate Section 24. Next locate the northwest ¼ of Section 24. Subdivide the quarter section into four quarters and locate the southeast ¼ of that subdivision.

Example: Locate the N½ of the NE¼ of the SE¼ of Section 12.
                              (3)   (2)   (1)

1. Locate the SE¼.

2. Locate the NE¼ of the SE¼.

3. Locate the N½ of the NE¼ of
   the SE¼.

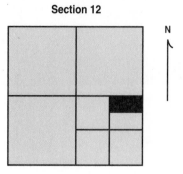

Section 12

N

PRACTICE PROBLEMS

3. Locate the NE¼ of the SE¼
   of the NW¼ of Section 36.

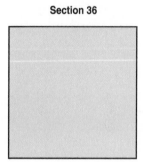

Section 36

CALCULATING NUMBER OF ACRES

To determine the number of acres in a tract, either of two approaches can be used:

1. Take 640 (the number of acres in one section) and divide by each of the
   denominators in the legal description. For example:

   NE¼, SE¼, NW¼ of Section 36

   $640 \div 4 \div 4 \div 4 = 10$ acres

2. Multiply the denominators of each fraction together and then divide 640 by
   the result. For example:

   NE¼, SE¼, NW¼ of Section 36

   Denominators: $4 \times 4 \times 4 = 64$

   640 acres $\div 64 = 10$ acres

As you can see, either method yields identical results. Choose the method that
you prefer and memorize the procedure.

> **Hint:** The answer will be identical regardless of whether you enter
> the numbers in the legal from left to right or right to left. Some
> students prefer to always work backwards from the section
> number (right to left) because this order is necessary when
> *locating* a parcel from a legal description. (Refer to page 48.)

4. How many acres are contained in a tract described as SW¼ of the NE¼ of Section 3?

_____

5. How many acres are contained in a tract described as N½ of the SW¼ of the SE¼ of Section 6?

_____

6. How many acres are contained in a tract described as E½ of the NW¼ of the SE¼ of the SE¼ of Section 21?

_____

7. How many acres are contained in a tract described as the W½ of the E½ of the NW¼ of Section 2?

_____

Calculating Number of Acres with "and" in the Description

When a legal description contains the word _and,_ calculate the number of acres and stop on reaching 'and,' Begin a new calculation on the other side of the 'and.' Conclude by adding the two acreages.

Example: How many acres are contained in a tract described as the S½, SW¼, SE¼ Section 6 and the N½, NW¼, NE¼ Section 7?

$$\text{Section } 6 = 2 \times 4 \times 4 = 32 \quad 640 \div 32 = 20 \text{ acres}$$

$$\text{Section } 7 = 2 \times 4 \times 4 = 32 \quad 640 \div 32 = 20 \text{ acres}$$

$$\text{Total acres in tract: } 20 + 20 = 40 \text{ acres}$$

Or alternatively:

$$640 \div 2 \div 4 \div 4 = 20 \text{ acres}$$

$$640 \div 2 \div 4 \div 4 = 20 \text{ acres}$$

$$\text{Total acres in tract: } 20 + 20 = 40 \text{ acres}$$

8. How many acres are included in a property described as NW¼ of the SE¼ and S½ of the SW¼ of the NE¼ of Section 23?

_____

9. How many acres are contained in the E½ of the NE¼ and the NW¼ of the S½ of the NE¼ of section 36?

_____

Converting Square Feet to Acres

To find the exact number of acres in a parcel where square feet are involved, divide the number of square feet by 43,560 square feet. This is the most commonly used method for converting square feet to acres.

Because more mistakes seem to be made when dividing than when multiplying, the *factor-of-23 method* may be helpful. This method uses 23 because one square foot is approximately .000023 of an acre (1 sq. ft. ÷ 43,560 sq. ft. = approximately .000023). This procedure avoids dividing entirely and is accurate to 1/100 of one acre. However, as the number of acres increases, the accuracy decreases.

Step 1   Determine the number of square feet involved.

Step 2   Multiply the total number of square feet by 23.

Step 3   Place a decimal point six places to the left of the last digit in the answer.

In the following example, the two methods are shown. Compare their accuracy.

Example: Calculate the number of acres in a tract that measures 460' × 490'.

$$460' \times 490' = 225,400 \text{ sq. ft.}$$

225,400 sq. ft. ÷ 43,560 sq. ft./acre	225,400 sq. ft. × 23
= 5.1744719 acres	= 5184200
= 5.2 acres (rounded)	= 5 184200.
	= 5.2 acres (rounded)

Hint: Many students recall the convenience store chain Seven-11 to help remember the number of square feet in an acre: 4 + 3 = 7 and 5 + 6 = 11. So think '7-11' to recall 43,560 square feet in an acre!

PRACTICE PROBLEMS

10.   How many acres are there in 44,500 square feet?

_____

11.   How many acres are there in 140,400 square feet?

_____

Referring to the diagram of Section 4 below, write the legal description and then determine the number of acres in each of the eight lettered areas of Section 4.

	Legal Description	**Number of Acres**
12. (a)		
13. (b)		
14. (c)		
15. (d)		
16. (e)		
17. (f)		
18. (g)		
19. (h)		

Section 4

20. Ms. Duval wants to buy a parcel measuring 1,935 × 1,800. If neighboring land has recently sold for $800 per acre, how much should Ms. Duval expect to pay? (Round the number of acres to the nearest whole acre.)

21. Mr. Walton owned the SW¼ of a section. He sold the E½ of that SW¼. How many acres does Mr. Walton still own?

22. The city aviation authority bought a tract of farmland described as the S½ of the N½ of the SE¼ of Section 8. A total of $640,000 was paid for the land. What was the cost per acre?

SOLVING MULTISTEP SQUARE FOOTAGE PROBLEMS

Students may be required to convert units of measurement *before* calculating square feet or acres.

Example: A lot measures 250 feet by 150 yards. The lot sells for $56,250. What is the sale price per square foot?

Step 1   Begin by converting yards into feet. There are 3 feet in a single yard, therefore:

$$150 \text{ yards} \times 3 = 450 \text{ feet}$$

Step 2   Now we see that the dimensions of the lot are 250 feet by 450 feet. The problem asks for sale price per square foot. Our next step is to calculate the number of square feet in the parcel.

$$250 \times 450 = 112,500 \text{ square feet}$$

Step 3   Sale price ÷ square feet = price per square foot
$56,250 sale price ÷ 112,500 square feet =
$0.50 per square foot

23.   A lot measures 110 yards wide by 300 feet deep. How many acres are contained in the parcel?

_____

24.   A parcel is ½ mile wide and 2,000 feet deep. A neighboring property sold for $2,250 per acre. How much should this property sell for?

_____

25.   A parcel contains 50 acres. The owner wants to subdivide part of the parcel into 20 lots measuring 100 feet by 217.8 feet. How many acres will be subdivided?

_____

SOLVING AREA AND VOLUME PROBLEMS

To determine the area of any tract, the general shape must be known (square, triangle, and so forth). When a legal description is involved, it must be read carefully. It is best to sketch the boundaries described as near to scale as possible to reveal the shape of the tract and apply the correct formula for the shape involved.

The area of four-sided square and rectangular parcels is calculated by taking the length times the width. The term **per front foot** is the number of feet of frontage of the lot. When dimensions are given, the number of front feet is always given first, followed by the depth of the lot.

Example: A parcel of land is for sale at $5,000 per front foot. What will it cost to purchase the parcel if the dimensions are 150 feet by 100 feet?

The parcel has frontage of 150 feet, therefore:
$5,000 per front foot × 150 = $750,000 cost of lot

The area within a parcel of land is expressed in square feet or in acres. Area is calculated by multiplying the parcel's length times its width.

Alternatively, you may remember from high school geometry the terms _base_ and _height._

Area of a Square or Rectangle
Area = Base × Height
_Or:_
Area = Length × Width

Example: How many acres are in a parcel of land that measures 450 feet × 484 feet?

450 feet × 484 feet = 217,800 square feet
217,800 square feet ÷ 43,560 = 5 acres

26. The front and back boundaries of a parcel are parallel to each other. Both are 400 feet long. The two sides are also parallel and also 400 feet long. How many acres are contained in the property?

The **perimeter** of a parcel is the linear distance around each side of the parcel. It is the total length around each side of the parcel.

Example: A rectangular lot measures 50 feet by 150 feet. The perimeter of the lot measures how many linear feet?

50 ft.

150 ft.

50 + 150 + 50 + 150 = 400 linear feet

27. What is the perimeter of (distance around) a township?

AREA PROBLEMS INVOLVING TRIANGLES

For all triangles, use the following formula:

Area of a Triangle
Area = ½(Base × Height)

Example: How many square feet are in a three-sided tract of land that is 300 feet on the base and 400 feet high?

Area = ½(300 × 400)
Area = 120,000 square feet ÷ 2
Area = 60,000 square feet

Parcels, however, are not typically described as triangular in shape. Let's look at another example.

Example: The parcel of property located on the corner of Watson Avenue and Condor Street has a base side of 150 feet of frontage on Watson Avenue and a side of 100 feet parallel to Condor Street. The third side is 180.28 feet. How many acres are included in these boundaries?

By sketching the property boundaries at a street intersection, we see that the base side *(b)* is the boundary line paralleling Watson Avenue. From this point, sketch in the boundary on Condor Street, which turns out to be the height boundary *(h)*. The third boundary merely connects the two previously described boundaries. When you see the shape of the property, you know which formula to apply.

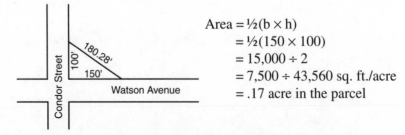

Area = ½(b × h)
    = ½(150 × 100)
    = 15,000 ÷ 2
    = 7,500 ÷ 43,560 sq. ft./acre
    = .17 acre in the parcel

> **Hint:** While the same procedure and the same formula apply to any three-sided tract of property, remember that the height is the perpendicular distance from the base to the highest point.

Example: A tract of land is 200 feet on its base side. Two other boundary lines are each 165.6 feet long and extend from the two ends of the base side to a point where they intersect exactly 132 feet from the midpoint of the base side. How many acres are contained within the boundaries?

Sketching the base line first and connecting two lines, one from each end of the base side forms a triangle with two sides equal in length.

The height *(h)* must be the perpendicular distance from the base *(b)* to the highest point. In this case the intersection of the two lines is the highest point. The distance from that point of intersection to the base side is 132 feet, so *h* is 132 feet and *b* is 200 feet.

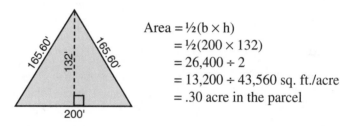

Area = ½(b × h)
     = ½(200 × 132)
     = 26,400 ÷ 2
     = 13,200 ÷ 43,560 sq. ft./acre
     = .30 acre in the parcel

PRACTICE PROBLEMS

28. The base side of a triangular parcel is 726 feet. The other sides are each 500 feet. The height at which the two sides meet is 300 feet in length vertically from the base. How many acres are in the parcel?

Example: A residential lot on Lake Maitland is 150 feet on one parallel side and 120 feet on the opposite parallel side. The west boundary of the lot is 110 feet and joins the parallel sides at an angle of 90 degrees on both sides. How many acres are in the lot?

Sketch the lot from the description. Because one parallel side is longer than the other (150' versus 120') and because they are joined at one side by a line forming two 90-degree angles, you can produce a figure somewhat as follows. Once you see the shape of the lot, you know to use the formula for the area of a trapezoid (a four-sided figure with only two sides parallel and four angles). Notice that we basically have a figure that consists of a rectangle and a triangle. Rather than memorize another formula we can calculate the area of the two shapes and add them together. Let's begin with the area of the rectangle (area *R*). Use the base that is shorter in length.

Area = (b × h)
     = (110 × 120)
     = 13,200 square feet

We can see from our diagram that the height of the triangle is 110 feet. The base is simply the difference between the longer base and the shorter base, or 150 – 120 = 30 feet.

$$
\begin{aligned}
\text{Area T} &= (b \times h) \div 2 \\
&= (110 \times 30) \div 2 \\
&= 3,300 \div 2 \\
&= 1,650 \text{ square feet}
\end{aligned}
$$

The total area of our parcel is:

13,200 square feet + 1,650 square feet = 14,850 square feet.

Lastly, we need to divide this figure by 43,560 to determine the number of acres in the parcel.

14,850 ÷ 43,560 = .34 acres

PRACTICE PROBLEMS

29. How many acres are in the parcel described as, "From the POB proceed due West 2,000 feet, thence South 575 feet, then due East 2,250 feet, and then returning to the POB."

It is not unusual to find that the shape of a parcel of real property does not conform to that of a square, rectangle, triangle, and so forth. When this occurs, it is normally possible to divide the parcel into a series of figures that conform to common shapes.

Example: Refer to the diagram. What is the total area of the parcel of land in square feet?

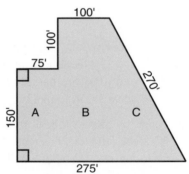

The above parcel can be divided into three common geometric figures: two rectangles and one triangle:

rectangle A: 150' × 75' =	11,250 sq. ft.
rectangle B: 250' × 100' =	25,000 sq. ft.
triangle C: (100' × 250') ÷ 2 =	+ 12,500 sq. ft.
total area of parcel =	48,750 sq. ft.

FORMULAS TO USE IN CUBIC MEASURE (VOLUME) PROBLEMS

From time to time, it is necessary to determine the volume of a room or building. Volume is always expressed in cubic units (cubic inches, cubic feet, and so forth).

To calculate volume, one step of computation is added to the calculation of area. It involves a third dimension, in addition to the dimensions required to find area.

To find the volume (cubic measure) of all squares and rectangles, use the following:

FORMULA

Volume

Length × Width × Height = Volume

Example: You want to build a swimming pool 16 feet by 54 feet by 9 feet. How many cubic yards of earth must be excavated to provide the space for the pool?

$$Volume = length \times width \times height$$
$$= 54' \times 16' \times 9'$$
$$= 7,776 \text{ cubic feet}$$
$$= 7,776 \text{ cubic feet} \div 27 \text{ (cu. ft./cu. yd.)}$$
$$= 288 \text{ cubic yards of earth}$$

COST PER UNIT

Quite often, a real estate practitioner must determine the cost per square foot or the cost per acre of a parcel of real property.

Example: If the cost of a 57,575-square-foot residential lot is $23,030, what is the cost per square foot?

$$Cost = sale\ price \div total\ square\ footage$$
$$= \$23,030 \div 57,575 \text{ square feet}$$
$$= \$.40 \text{ per square foot}$$

The same procedure is utilized to compute the cost per acre.

$$Cost = sale\ price \div number\ of\ acres$$
$$= \$23,030 \div (57,575 \text{ sq. ft.} \div 43,560 \text{ sq. ft. per acre})$$
$$= \$23,030 \div 1.3217401 \text{ acres}$$
$$= \$17,424 \text{ per acre}$$

> **Hint:** Acres or square feet are always divided into dollars because we are looking for dollars per unit of something. Most errors occur when the reverse is done.

30. A waterfront lot measures 150 feet by 200 feet. The owner has offered it for sale at $40,500. Calculate the asking price per square foot.

_____

31. A lot's dimensions are 290 × 750. The lot cost $32,670 per acre. What is the cost per square foot?

_____

32. An office suite measures 20 × 50 and rents for $2,000 per month. What is the rent per square foot per year for the office suite?

_____

MULTISTEP AREA PROBLEMS

Sometimes students may encounter a word problem that asks for something other than the number of square feet or the cost per acre. Often these are square foot problems but are worded in such a way that it might not be readily apparent.

Example: A contractor plans to construct a four-story office building with 8,000 square feet of space per floor. Zoning regulations require one parking space for every 400 square feet of building area. How many parking spaces are required?

Step 1   Begin by calculating the total square footage:

8,000 square feet per floor × 4 floors = 32,000 square feet

Step 2   Divide the total square feet by 400 to determine required parking spaces:

32,000 ÷ 400 = 80 parking spaces

You may find that applying principles that you learned in high school algebra can help you solve complicated word problems.

Example: A buyer acquired three lots for a total price of $74,000. If the second lot cost $4,000 more than the first lot, and the third lot cost $6,000 more than the second lot, what was the cost of the first lot?

We know that the cost of the three lots combined is $74,000. Let the letter x represent the cost of lot 1:

$$x = \text{lot 1}$$
$$x + \$4,000 = \text{lot 2}$$
$$x + \$4,000 + \$6,000 = \text{lot 3}$$

So we can rewrite this as follows:

$$x + x + x + \$4,000 + \$4,000 + \$6,000 = \$74,000$$

Let's rewrite our statement by doing the addition on the left hand side of the equal sign:

$$3x + \$14,000 = \$74,000$$

To solve for x (the cost of lot 1) we need to isolate x on one side of the equal sign. We can subtract $14,000 from each side of the equal sign to get x by itself:

$$3x + 14,000 - 14,000 = \$74,000 - \$14,000$$
$$3x = \$60,000$$

But x is still not by itself. We have $3x$ on the left side of the equal sign. $3x$ is the same as 3 times x. So to get the x by itself we can do the opposite of multiply; we can divide each side of the equal sign by 3.

$$3 \div 3 = 1, \text{ and } 1x \text{ is the same as just } x$$
$$x = \$60,000 \div 3$$
$$x = \$20,000$$

So:

$$\begin{aligned}
\text{Lot 1 cost} \quad &= \$20,000 \\
\text{Lot 2 cost } \$20,000 + \$4,000 \quad &= \$24,000 \\
\text{Lot 3 cost } \$24,000 + \$6,000 \quad &= \$30,000
\end{aligned}$$

If we calculated the cost of lot 1 correctly, the three lots should total $74,000:

$$\$20,000 + \$24,000 + \$30,000 = \$74,000 \text{ Yippee!}$$

PRACTICE PROBLEMS

33. The cost of three lots is $61,000. The second lot cost $5,000 more than the first lot, and the third lot cost $6,000 more than the second lot. What is the cost of the first lot?

_____

34. A contractor builds a two-story warehouse measuring 120×150. Ten percent of the space is allocated to elevators and landings. The contractor plans to store bins of construction material that each measure 10×12.

a. How many bins will the building accommodate?

_____

b. If the bins rent for $6.00 per month, what is the annual income?

_____

35. A lot measures 120×150. If zoning regulations require a 15-foot setback from the street, what are the buildable dimensions of the lot?

_____

ANSWER KEY

1.

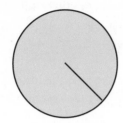

2. 200 feet × 200 feet = 40,000 square feet

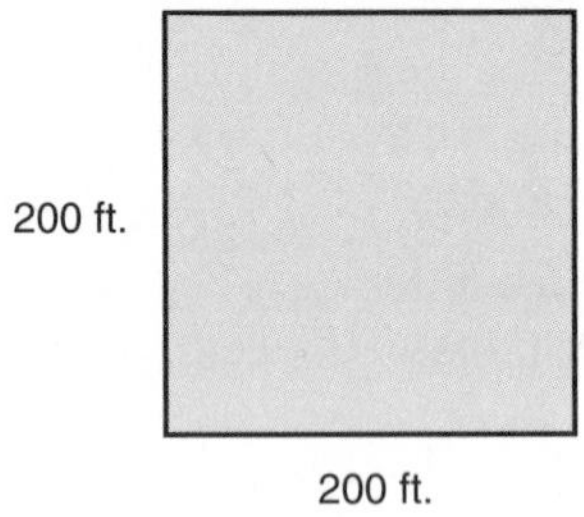

200 ft.

200 ft.

3.

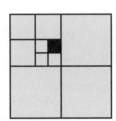

4. 640 ÷ 4 ÷ 4 = 40 acres

5. 640 ÷ 2 ÷ 4 ÷ 4 = 20 acres

6. 640 ÷ 2 ÷ 4 ÷ 4 ÷ 4 = 5 acres

7. 640 ÷ 2 ÷ 2 ÷ 4 = 40 acres

8. 640 acres ÷ 4 ÷ 4 = 40 acres;
640 ÷ 2 ÷ 4 ÷ 4 = 20 acres;
40 + 20 = 60 acres

9. 640 ÷ 2 ÷ 4 = 80 acres;
640 ÷ 4 ÷ 2 ÷ 4 = 20 acres;
80 + 20 = 100 acres

10. 44,500 square feet ÷ 43,560 =
1.02158 or 1.02 acres (rounded)

11. 140,400 sq. ft. ÷ 43,560 =
3.22314 or 3.2 acres (rounded)

12. SW¼; 640 acres ÷ 4 = 160 acres

13. SE¼, NW¼;
640 acres ÷ 4 = 160 acres;
160 acres ÷ 4 = 40 acres

14. N½, NW¼;
640 acres ÷ 4 = 160 acres;
160 acres ÷ 2 = 80 acres

15. N½, SW¼, NW¼;
640 acres ÷ 4 = 160 acres;
160 acres ÷ 4 = 40 acres;
40 acres ÷ 2 = 20 acres

16. W½, E½, NE¼;
640 acres ÷ 4 = 160 acres;
160 ÷ 2 = 80 acres;
80 acres ÷ 2 = 40 acres

17. W½, W½, NE¼, SE¼;
640 acres ÷ 4 = 160 acres;
160 ÷ 4 = 40 acres;
40 acres ÷ 2 = 20 acres;
20 ÷ 2 = 10 acres

18. SE¼, SW¼, SE¼;
640 acres ÷ 4 = 160 acres;
160 ÷ 4 = 40 acres;
40 acres ÷ 4 = 10 acres

19. SE¼, SE¼;
640 acres ÷ 4 = 160 acres;
160 ÷ 4 = 40 acres

20. 1,935 × 1,800 = 3,483,000 square feet;
3,483,000 ÷ 43,560 = 79.96 or 80 (rounded) acres;
80 acres × $800/acre = $64,000

21. 640 acres ÷ 4 = 160 acres in a quarter section;
160 ÷ 2 = 80 acres

22. 640 acres ÷ 4 ÷ 4 ÷ 2 = 40 acres;
$640,000 ÷ 40 acres = $16,000 per acre

23. 110 yards × 3 = 330 feet;
330 × 300 = 99,000 square feet;
99,000 ÷ 43,560 = 2.27 acres

24. 5,280 feet = 1 mile; 5,280 ÷ 2 =
2,640 feet = the parcel's width;
2,640 × 2,000 = 5,280,000 square feet;
5,280,000 square feet ÷ 43,560 =
121.21212 acres;
$2,250 × 121.21212 =
$272,727.27 projected sale price

25. 100 × 217.8 = 21,780 square feet;
21,780 square feet × 20 lots =
435,600 square feet;
435,600 ÷ 43,560 = 10 acres

26. a = b × h;
400 × 400 = 160,000 square feet;
160,000 square feet ÷ 43,560 = 3.67 acres

27. 6 miles + 6 miles + 6 miles + 6 miles =
24 miles perimeter

28. Area of a triangle: (726 base × 300 height) ÷ 2;
217,800 ÷ 2 = 108,900;
108,900 ÷ 43,560 = 2.5 acres

29. Area of a rectangle: 2,000 × 575 =
1,150,000 square feet;
Area of a triangle: (250 × 575) ÷ 2;
143,750 ÷ 2 = 71,875;
1,150,000 + 71,875 = 1,221,875 ÷ 43,560 =
28.05 acres

30. 150 × 200 = 30,000 square feet:
$40,500 asking price ÷ 30,000 square feet =
$1.35 per square foot

31. $32,680 ÷ 43,560 = $.75 per square foot
(Note: lot dimensions were not relevant to solving
this problem)

32. 20 × 50 = 1,000 square feet;
$2,000 rent × 12 months = $24,000 rent per year;
$24,000 ÷ 1,000 =
$24 per square foot rent per year

33. x = lot 1; x + 5,000 = lot 2;
x + $5,000 + $6,000 = lot 3;
x + x + x + $5,000 + $5,000 + $6,000 = $61,000;
$3x$ + $16,000 = $61,000;
$3x$ + $16,000 − $16,000 = $61,000 − $16,000;
$3x$ = $45,000;
3 ÷ $3x$ = $45,000 ÷ 3;
x = $15,000 cost of lot 1

34. (a):
120 × 150 × 2 stories = 36,000 total square feet;
36,000 × .90 = 32,400 available for bin storage;
10 × 12 = 120 square feet for each bin;
32,400 ÷ 120 = 270 bins
(b):
270 bins × $6.00 × 12 months =
$19,440 annual income

35. 120 is the lot's frontage.
150 − 15 foot setback from the street = 135;
120 × 135 = buildable lot dimensions

Chapter Five

MORTGAGE MATH

KEY TERMS

Amortized Mortgage a mortgage in which periodic payments cover both interest on the outstanding balance and a partial repayment of principal

Assumption of Mortgage the taking over of an existing mortgage by a buyer

Doc Stamp Tax Notes tax required on promissory notes (in some states)

Intangible Tax tax required prior to recording a new mortgage (in some states)

Interest (I) the cost of using someone else's money (or the amount you receive for lending your money)

Mortgage a written agreement that pledges real property as security for payment of a debt

Principal (P) the amount of money borrowed (or the amount loaned by a lender)

Rate of Interest (R) the annual percent that must be paid to use the money

Time (T) the term or duration a borrower has use of money expressed in years (or part of a year)

Chapter | **Overview**

The vast majority of all real estate transactions involve financing. This loaning (and borrowing) of money has prompted the creation of financial terminology. In this chapter we review the calculations associated with financing.

> **Hint:** When any three elements in a mortgage problem are known, the fourth element can always be calculated. The following formulas apply:
>
> *where:* P = principal; R = rate of interest; T = time; and I = interest.
>
> $$I = P \times R \times T \qquad P = \frac{I}{R \times T} \qquad R = \frac{I}{P \times T} \qquad T = \frac{I}{P \times R}$$

All of these formulas are incorporated into a T-device, as explained later in this chapter.

CALCULATING INTEREST

Most people would not stop to figure the actual rate of interest if offered a loan of $100 at a cost of $1 per week. Yet over a period of one year, this would mean paying $52 in interest, which is a 52 percent annual rate of interest! However, if the interest were $1 per *month,* the annual rate would be a more acceptable 12 percent.

While interest is usually charged monthly, interest rates are normally expressed as a yearly (annual) rate. When dealing with interest problems involving a single year, the calculation of interest is straightforward.

Example: What is the interest on $10,000 at 8 percent per year for 1 year?

$$\begin{aligned}
\text{Interest} &= \text{principal} \times \text{rate} \times \text{time} \\
&= \$10,000 \times 8\% \text{ per year} \times 1 \text{ year} \\
&= \$10,000 \times .08 \times 1 \\
&= \$800
\end{aligned}$$

In dealing with time, all calculations are related to a one-year period:

Annual interest = principal × rate

Monthly interest = annual interest ÷ 12

Daily interest[1] = annual interest ÷ 365

or, if prorating a single month,

Monthly interest ÷ number of days in the month of concern

---

[1] In states that use the 360/30-Day Method, Daily interest = annual interest ÷ 360 days or, if prorating for a single month, monthly interest ÷ 30 days.

> **Hint:** Answers will be more accurate if figures are carried out to at least three places to the right of the decimal point and at least three decimal places are kept until the final answer. Round off the final answer to two decimal places.

Example: What amount of interest must be paid on $10,000 at 9½ percent for four months and seven days?

$$\text{Annual interest} = \$10,000 \times .095 = \$950$$
$$\text{Monthly interest} = \$950 \div 12 = \$79.167$$
$$\text{Daily interest} = \$950 \div 365 = \$2.603$$

$$4 \text{ months} = 4 \times \$79.167 = \quad \$316.668$$
$$7 \text{ days} = 7 \times \$2.603 = \underline{+ \ \$ \ \ 18.221}$$
$$\$334.889 \text{ or } \$334.89 \text{ (rounded)}$$

USING TIME IN THE T-DEVICE

Interest is always the result of an amount owed **(principal)** multiplied by a **rate of interest** multiplied by a part of a year **(time).** The first three terms—interest (*part*), principal (*total*), and rate of interest (*rate*)—fit easily into the memory aid. However, to solve mortgage problems, the aid must be modified to include the fourth term—*time*—a very important factor in money lending:

Time Chart
2 years = 2
1 year = 1
18 months = 1.5
9 months = .75
6 months = .5 (6 months divided by 12)
3 months = .25
1 month = .0833

FORMULA

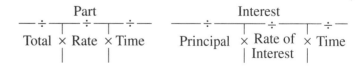

The amount of interest always should be placed over the horizontal line of the memory device (*part*). Interest is a form of income, therefore, when a problem does not mention interest but does refer to income, the amount of income should be placed above the horizontal line of the modified diagram.

In these four-element problems, perform all the multiplication first, then the division. (In any equation in which parentheses appear, first perform the arithmetic operation within the parentheses.)

Example: What is the principal amount borrowed if a 9 percent rate of interest results in payment of $135 interest for a period of six months?

Principal = $135 ÷ (9% × 6 months)

= $135 ÷ (.09 × .5)

= $135 ÷ .045

= $3,000

$$\frac{}{?}÷\frac{\$135}{×\quad 9\%}÷\frac{}{×\,6\text{ months}}÷\frac{}{}$$

Hint: Time must be expressed in years, or portions of years, because interest rates are understood to be annual rates (unless otherwise indicated).

Example: How long did a borrower have use of $42,000 if a 9½ percent rate of interest cost her $9,975?

Time = $9,975 ÷ ($42,000 × 9½%)

= $9,975 ÷ ($42,000 × .095)

= $9,975 ÷ $3,990

= 2.5 years, or 2½ years, or 2 years and 6 months

$$\frac{}{\$42,000}÷\frac{\$9,975}{×\quad 9½\%}÷\frac{}{×\quad ?}÷\frac{}{}$$

Suppose she had paid only $997.50 in interest with the same borrowed amount and interest rate as above. How long would she have had the use of the loan?

Time = $997.50 ÷ ($42,000 × .095)

= $997.50 ÷ $3,990

= .25 years, or 3 months

$$\frac{}{\$42,000}÷\frac{\$997.50}{×\quad 9½\%}÷\frac{}{×\quad ?}÷\frac{}{}$$

PRACTICE PROBLEMS

1. On a $3,000 loan for six months, $146.25 was paid as interest. What was the rate of interest?

2. What is the amount of interest on a $68,000 (interest-only) mortgage at an 11.6 percent rate for nine months?

3. On a $2,000 loan with a 9 percent interest rate, $60 interest was paid. How long was the term of the loan?

4. A borrower has a straight term mortgage at 6 percent annual interest. The borrower is required to make a semiannual interest payment of $900. How much does the borrower owe?

MORTGAGE FINANCIAL PACKAGES

A **mortgage** financial package includes the computation of the (1) *down payment;* (2) *loan amount;* (3) *discount points;* (4) *taxes on the mortgage,* where applicable; and (5) the *total monthly payment,* to include principal, interest, taxes, and insurance (PITI). In some instances, the broker or sales associate may need to prepare a financial package comparing figures for several loan plans, including fixed-rate and adjustable-rate mortgages.

The minimum down payment required will depend on the type of financing arranged—FHA, VA, or conventional mortgage loan. Let's discuss the various computations for each type of mortgage loan, begining with conventional mortgages.

Conventional Mortgage Loan Down Payments

Conventional mortgage loans generally vary from 50 percent to 95 percent of total value. Private mortgage insurance (PMI) arrangements may permit a buyer to pay as little as 3 percent of the sale price or appraised value (whichever is lower) as a down payment. However, conventional mortgages normally require a larger down payment compared with government-sponsored loans. Most lenders require PMI when more than 80 percent is borrowed.

Whatever the percent of selling price required as a down payment, proper use of the memory aid indicates the operation needed to calculate the amount of down payment required for a conventional loan.

Selling price = *total*

Percent required as down payment = *rate*

Amount of down payment = *part*

FORMULA

Amount of Down Payment

Selling price × Percent required down = Down payment

Example: What is the down payment for a house appraised at $84,000 and requiring a 20% down payment?

$84,000 × .20 = $16,800 down payment

PRACTICE PROBLEMS

5. You are a broker and have placed in escrow a 10 percent earnest money deposit on the appraised value of a house. A mortgage company has agreed to lend the buyer $58,800, which is 80 percent of the appraised value of the property. How much earnest money do you have in escrow?

6. A buyer has made an earnest money deposit of $5,000 on a home selling for $79,500. A bank has agreed to lend the buyer 75 percent of the sale price. How much additional cash must the buyer furnish to complete the required down payment?

7. The sale price of a home is $89,700. A savings institution will finance 90 percent of the purchase price. How much will the buyer be required to pay as a down payment?

_____

8. A buyer has agreed to pay 10 percent down on a home selling for $71,500. A mortgage has been arranged for the balance of the purchase price. The buyer has agreed to pay 1½ percent of the loan amount at closing for prepaid private mortgage insurance. How much money must the buyer bring to the closing if she has already paid an earnest money deposit of $1,000?

_____

Conventional Loan Amounts

As indicated earlier, lenders making conventional loans may lend up to 95 percent of the appraised value. The maximum available amount of a conventional loan, therefore, typically varies from 50 percent to 95 percent of the appraised value. A survey of local lenders will disclose the maximum loan available.

Example: How much money will a lender loan if a property has been appraised at $104,500 and the buyer/borrower is required to invest an amount equal to 20 percent of the property value?

Available Loan

Appraised value – Required investment = Available loan

$100\% - 20\% = 80\%$

$104,500 \times .80 = \$83,600$ available loan

9. The newspaper advertises a condominium selling for $69,700 with 95% financing and no closing costs. How much loan will the buyer be allowed if the minimum down payment is made?

_____

VA Mortgage Loans

Only veterans, surviving spouses of veterans, and active military personnel may apply for a VA loan. The VA establishes loan guarantee limits referred to as the *VA loan guarantee* or the *maximum entitlement*. Currently, the maximum entitlement (guarantee) is $89,912.

A veteran begins by applying to the VA for a certificate of eligibility. The *certificate of eligibility* states the amount of entitlement available to the veteran. The entitlement is based on the loan amount.

VA Home Loan Guarantee Entitlement	
Loan Amount	**Guaranteed Amount**
0 to $45,000	50 percent of the loan amount
$45,001 to $144,000	Minimum guaranty is $22,500 with a maximum guaranty of up to 40 percent of the loan up to $36,000
More than $144,000	Up to $89,912 or 25 percent of the loan amount

Because the maximum loan guaranty is $89,912, the maximum loan amount with *no down payment* is $359,650 ($89,912 × 4). No maximum loan amount has been established for VA loans, except that the loan cannot exceed the appraised value of the home as estimated by a VA-approved appraiser and stated in the Certificate of Reasonable Value (CRV). The other limiting factor is the veteran's income and ability to make monthly mortgage payments consisting of principal, interest, tax, and insurance payments (PITI).

The VA requires a *funding fee* or *user's fee* to help the government defray the cost of foreclosures. The funding fee may be added to the maximum loan amount and financed as long as the total loan does not exceed $359,650. Alternatively, the fee may be paid at closing. The funding fee is a percentage of the mortgage amount, depending on how many times the veteran has used the benefit. If the veteran has a service-connected disability, the funding fee is waived.

The veteran borrower's total monthly obligation may not exceed 41 percent of total monthly gross income. A veteran borrower's total monthly obligation consists of the mortgage payment (principal, interest, taxes, and insurance or PITI) plus other long-term debt divided by monthly gross income. The procedure for calculating the percentage of total monthly obligations is explained later in this chapter.

FHA 203(b) Program and Down Payment Amounts

The FHA Down Payment Simplification Act of 2002 amended the National Housing Act to permanently simplify the down payment requirements for FHA-insured mortgages for single-family homebuyers. The maximum FHA mortgage amount for a FHA residential loan is based on a fixed percentage of sale price or the appraised value, whichever is less. The FHA has developed two sets of percentages—one for low closing cost states and the other for high closing cost states. Most states are classified as high closing cost states. The percentages for calculating the maximum loan amount in high closing cost states are presented below.

FHA Percentages for High Closing Cost States	
98.75%	Equal to or less than $50,000 sale price (or appraised value)
97.75%	More than $50,000

Example: Assume the sale price and appraised value of a home is $44,000. What is the maximum FHA loan amount in a high closing cost state?

$44,000 sale price × .9875 = $43,450 maximum FHA loan amount

The $43,450 figure is the maximum that FHA will insure *provided* the borrower (mortgagor) makes a *cash investment* of at least 3 percent. The 3 percent cash requirement is calculated on the lesser of the purchase price or appraised value. Let's calculate the buyer's minimum cash investment:

$44,000 sale price × .03 = $1,320 minimum cash investment

If the buyer is paying closing costs, they may be applied toward satisfying the 3 percent requirement.

Example: Assume the buyer in the previous example has closing costs totaling $700. Because the buyer is paying $700 in closing costs, the total acquisition cost of the property is the sale price plus the closing costs:

$44,000 sale price + $700 buyer closing costs = $44,700 total acquisition cost

The maximum FHA loan amount calculated earlier was $43,450 leaving a difference of $1,250 ($44,700 total acquisition cost – $43,450 maximum loan amount = $1,250). However, the minimum cash investment calculated earlier was $1,320. Therefore, the loan amount must be reduced by $70 to ensure that the buyer invests at least 3 percent ($1,320) into the property.

The required investment must be from the borrower's own funds, a bona fide gift, a loan from a family member, or from a governmental agency. The money may not come from premium pricing, loans from other sources, the seller, or the builder.

To summarize, there are three steps involved in determining the FHA loan amount:

Step 1 Calculate the maximum FHA loan amount.

Step 2 Calculate the minimum cash investment using the purchase price or appraised value, whichever is less.

Step 3 If the buyer is paying closing costs, calculate the total acquisition cost. Compare the calculated down payment, including closing costs, to the minimum cash investment and adjust the loan amount, if necessary.

Example: Assume the property sold for and is appraised at $100,000. The homebuyer is paying $1,000 in closing costs.

Step 1 Calculate the maximum FHA loan amount:

$100,000 appraised value × .9775 =
$97,750 maximum FHA loan amount

Step 2 Calculate the minimum cash investment:

$100,000 × .03 = $3,000 minimum cash investment

Step 3 Compare:

$101,000 acquisition cost – $97,750 max loan amount =
$3,250 calculated down payment

Because the $3,250 represents at least 3 percent (greater than or equal to $3,000) of the sale price no further mortgage calculation is required. The FHA will insure up to $97,750 and the buyer's closing costs will total $3,250.

Lenders always make FHA-insured loans in even $50 increments. For example, if a loan calculates to $77,212, the lender is required to round the loan amount down to the next lower even $50 increment (in this case, $77,200). Rounding down increases the buyer's down payment by the amount dropped in rounding down (in this example, $12).

Note: The loan amounts have not been rounded down to even $50 increments in this book. For exam purposes, read the test question carefully to determine whether the loan amounts are to be rounded to even $50 increments.

PRACTICE PROBLEMS

Begin by practicing calculating the maximum loan amount and minimum cash investment for FHA loans. Assume the properties are located in a high closing cost state.

	Lesser of Appraised Value of Sale Price	**Maximum Loan Amount**	**Minimum Cash Investment**
10.	$44,500		
11.	$72,400		
12.	$92,000		

Now consider buyer's closing costs. You need to determine the total acquisition cost and compare the calculated down payment with the minimum cash investment. If the minimum cash investment has not been met, the loan amount must be adjusted.

13. Use the information in problem 10. Assume the buyer is paying closing costs of $800. What is the total acquisition cost? Does the loan amount need to be adjusted to meet the minimum cash investment requirement?

_____

14. Use the information in problem 11. Assume the buyer is paying closing costs of $500. What is the total acquisition cost? Does the loan amount need to be adjusted to meet the minimum cash investment requirement?

_____

15. Use the information in problem 12. Assume the buyer is paying closing costs of $1,000. What is the total acquisition cost? Does the loan amount need to be adjusted to meet the minimum cash investment requirement?

_____

MORTGAGE DISCOUNT POINTS

For years, extra charges called *mortgage discount points* were necessary to make the lower interest rates of federally sponsored mortgages competitive with the higher interest rates of conventional mortgage loans. As the money market reacted to increased demand, inflation, and a reduced supply of money, the character of discount points changed. Lenders now charge points as an interest "rate adjustment factor." In other words, the borrower is charged an up-front fee to increase the actual yield to the lender without showing an increase in the interest rate on the mortgage. The amount charged for the discount points is based on the loan amount.

Lenders use computers or prepared tables to determine the number of discount points that must be paid. However, as a general rule of thumb, each discount point paid to the lender will increase the lender's yield (return) by approximately ⅛ of 1 percent (.00125). In using the rule of thumb, for each discount point charged by a lender, add ⅛ percent to the stated (contract) mortgage interest rate to estimate the lender's real return (and cost to the borrower) from the loan.

> **Hint:** This rule-of-thumb calculation is designed to estimate the real (or effective) mortgage interest rate expressed as an annual percentage rate (APR), not as a dollar amount. The stated interest rate, as such, will not change.

To determine the actual cost, in dollars, added by discount points, each discount point is equal to 1 percent of the mortgage balance (1 point = 1 percent). The *mortgage balance* (loan amount) is multiplied by this discount percent to find the dollar amount of the discount being charged.

Example: Assume the market rate of interest is 8¼ percent and the FHA rate of interest is 7½ percent. The following steps should be used to approximate the discount points required to equal the market rate of interest and determine the amount of discount charged on a $60,000 FHA mortgage.

Step 1 Estimate the discount points required to raise the yield to the lender's required return:

1. Calculate the difference in the two rates.

Current market rate – stated (contract) interest rate = difference

$$8\tfrac{1}{4}\% - 7\tfrac{1}{2}\% = \tfrac{3}{4}\% \text{ difference}$$

2. Convert the difference to eighths of a percent.

$$\tfrac{3}{4}\% = \tfrac{6}{8}\%$$

3. Convert the eighths to discount points.

$$\tfrac{6}{8}\% \div \tfrac{1}{8}\% = 6 \text{ (discount points required)}$$

Step 2 Calculate the cost of discount points charged:

1. Convert discount points to discount rate.

$$6 \text{ points} \times 1\% \text{ per point} = 6\%$$

2. Calculate the amount of discount.

Total loan amount × discount rate = amount of discount

$$\$60,000 \times .06 = \$3,600 \text{ (cost of discount)}$$

With most loans, a borrower usually is not familiar with the above information. The more common experience is for the borrower or his or her agent to be told that a loan will require payment of 4 discount points, or 3, or 5, and so forth. The problem then is not only to calculate the cost of the discount points but also to determine the real yield to the lender.

Example: Using the same situation as above, assume that the need is to find the amount of yield to the lender if 6 discount points are charged for an FHA loan showing a contract rate of 7½ percent interest.

1. Convert discount points to percent of increase (1 point results in ⅛ of 1 percent increase).

$$6 \text{ points} \times \tfrac{1}{8}\% \text{ per point} = \tfrac{6}{8}\% \text{ increase}$$

2. Add to the contract rate the percent of increase.

$$7\tfrac{1}{2}\% + \tfrac{6}{8}\% = 8\tfrac{1}{4}\% \text{ (approximate yield to lender)}$$

When solving mortgage discount problems, remember that the cost of discount points is figured on the amount of the loan (1 discount point = 1 percent of the loan amount).

> **Hint:** Sometimes a lender will state that a mortgage is "going at" 98 or 96, for example. It means the same thing as quoting 2 discount points or 4 discount points.

PRACTICE PROBLEMS

16. A bank has agreed to lend $87,900 at 6½ percent interest for 30 years. The borrower is charged 2 discount points. How much will the borrower be required to pay for the discount points?

17. What is the approximate yield to the bank (cost to the borrower) in problem 16?

18. The FHA has agreed to insure a loan for the purchase of a new home selling for $77,500. An approved savings institution will make the actual loan at a 7 percent interest rate, but the borrower is to pay 4 discount points. How much will the discount points cost the borrower? (Assume a high closing cost state.)

19. What is the approximate yield to the lender (cost to the borrower) in problem 18?

20. A lender requires a yield of 8.25 percent interest, but has quoted an interest rate of 7.5 percent. How many points must the lender charge to obtain the required yield?

21. A builder has an FHA loan commitment of $63,000 on a house he is building. The bank will lend him $63,000 with 3 discount points to be charged when the house is financed. The builder decides to be safe and adds the equivalent of 4 points to the price of the house. How much did the 4 points increase the cost of the house over the loan commitment amount?

_____

22. A buyer has been approved for a 6½ percent FHA loan. FHA loans are currently going at a price of 95. What is the lender's true yield (APR) on this loan?

_____

23. A lender agrees to lend 80 percent of the appraised value of a condominium at a 6½ percent interest rate for 30 years. The condominium appraises for $125,000. The borrower is charged 2 discount points. Calculate the cost of the discount points.

_____

DEBT RATIOS

A debt ratio is the percentage of monthly income that can be applied toward monthly long-term obligations. Debt that cannot be paid off within 10 months is considered long-term debt. Loan programs have different guidelines on debt ratio percentages. FHA and VA loan programs have higher debt ratio percentages compared with conventional loans, allowing more homebuyers to qualify for government loan programs.

There are two types of debt ratios. One ratio is a housing expense ratio. It is concerned with the percentage of monthly income that can be applied toward monthly housing payments. The housing payment is made up of principal, interest, property taxes, and insurance (PITI). The PITI payment is divided by the borrower's monthly gross income to calculate the ratio:

FORMULA

Housing Expense Ratio

PITI ÷ Monthly gross income = Housing expense ratio

The *total obligations ratio* is the percentage of monthly income that can be applied toward all monthly long-term debt obligations. The PITI plus other monthly nonhousing long-term obligations (PITIO) are divided by the borrower's monthly gross income to calculate the ratio:

FORMULA

Total Obligations Ratio

PITIO ÷ Monthly gross income = Total obligations ratio

The following table indicates the debt to income ratios for FHA, VA, and conventional mortgage loans. VA uses a total monthly obligations ratio only. Conventional fixed rate and adjustable rate mortgages have the lowest debt to income ratios meaning that conventional mortgages require the most income in relation to long-term debt.

Debt Ratios		
	Housing Expense Ratio	**Total Monthly Obligations Ratio**
Conventional	28%	36%
FHA	29%	41%
VA		41%

Example: A couple has a combined gross monthly income of $3,600. They have applied for a VA-guaranteed loan of $150,000 at 7 percent for 30 years. Monthly payments of principal and interest total $997.95. Monthly payments of property taxes are $130 and $60 hazard insurance. Can they qualify for the loan if they have a car payment of $245?

Begin by determining the couple's total monthly expenses:

$997.95 principal and interest + $130 property taxes + $60 hazard insurance + $245 car payment = $1,432.95

Next apply the formula for calculating the total obligations ratio:

$1,432.95 total monthly debt ÷ $3,600 gross monthly income = .398 or 39.8%

The ratio of 39.8 percent does not exceed 41 percent so the couple qualifies for the loan.

PRACTICE PROBLEMS

24. Prospective borrowers want to know if they qualify for a conventional mortgage. They have an estimated PITI of $1,245 and a car payment of $450 per month. The couple has a combined monthly income of $3,300 per month. Does the couple's monthly housing expense qualify under the monthly housing expense ratio limit for conventional mortgage loans?

COMPUTING TRANSFER TAXES ON MORTGAGES

Many states have enacted laws that charge (levy) transfer taxes on instruments associated with debt, including promissory notes, mortgages, and deeds of trust. For example, in many states, two separate taxes must be paid each time a new mortgage is created.

1. A state **intangible tax** must be paid on new mortgages. This is a one-time tax (it is *not* paid annually). For instance, in some states, the tax rate is $.002 (two mills per dollar) multiplied by the amount of new indebtedness. (Check with your instructor to verify whether intangible tax applies in your state.)

2. A state **documentary stamp tax on the note** is paid as part of the mortgage package. For instance, in some states, the tax rate is $.35 per $100, or fractional part thereof, and is calculated on the face value of the note. This tax is a one-time tax and is due when the note is executed. (Check with your instructor to verify whether intangible tax applies in your state.)

In states that levy taxes on mortgages, every real estate transaction involving new financing reflects the cost of these taxes on closing statements. Sometimes an assumption of an existing mortgage is used to finance the purchase of real property. An **assumption of the mortgage** obligates the buyer to assume primary liability for the debt. If there is no change in the real property that secures the loan, a new mortgage is not created and therefore there would be no intangible taxes to pay. However, the note executed related to an assumed mortgage would be subject to a documentary stamp tax. Most states require that examinees demonstrate the ability to compute the amount of such taxes.

Example: Ms. Polk bought a home from Mr. and Mrs. Brevard for $79,500. The sale contract acknowledged receipt of a $3,800 earnest money deposit and specified that Ms. Polk was to assume a $32,000 existing mortgage. The Brevards were to take back a second mortgage in the amount of $30,000 in lieu of cash. Ms. Polk agreed to pay the balance of the purchase price in cash at closing. Using the above tax rates, what taxes would Ms. Polk pay if she has agreed to pay for the expenses associated with the new $30,000 second mortgage and the assumption?

Begin by calculating the intangible tax on the new mortgage:

$30,000 loan amount × $.002 tax rate = $60

Now calculate the documentary stamp tax on the note associated with the second mortgage:

$30,000 ÷ $100 increments = 300 taxable increments

300 taxable increments × $.35 tax rate = $105

Lastly, we must calculate the documentary stamp tax on the note associated with the assumption:

$32,000 ÷ $100 increments = 320 taxable increments

320 taxable increments × $.35 tax rate = $112

The total taxes to be paid are:

$60 + $105 + $112 = $277

Example: Mr. Dunn bought a condominium for $69,575. He paid an earnest money deposit of $2,000 and assumed an existing mortgage of $43,250; the seller took back a second mortgage in the amount of $24,325 in lieu of cash. What taxes on the new mortgages would Mr. Dunn pay if he contracted to pay all taxes created by the new loan and the assumption? Assume that the state levies taxes at the rates previously cited.

Intangible tax on the new mortgage:

$24,325 loan amount × $.002 tax rate = $48.65

Documentary stamp tax on the note associated with the second mortgage:

$24,325 ÷ $100 increments = 243.25 taxable increments
(.25 part requires the same tax as a whole increment;
change fractional part to 1 whole increment)

243 + 1 = 244 taxable increments

244 taxable increments × $.35 tax rate = $85.40

Documentary stamp tax on the note associated with the assumption:

$43,250 ÷ $100 increments = 432.5 taxable increments, rounded up to 433

433 taxable increments × $.35 tax rate = $151.55

Total taxes to be paid:

$48.65 + $85.40 + $151.55 = $285.60

PRACTICE PROBLEMS

Calculate the taxes required in the following situations, using the tax rates cited previously:

	New Mortgage Amount	Mortgage: Intangible Tax	Note: Documentary Stamp Tax
25.	$ 48,000		
26.	$ 87,000		
27.	$ 56,850		
28.	$ 92,760		
29.	$126,420		

COMPUTING MONTHLY PAYMENTS

The level monthly payment necessary to pay both principal and interest for various rates of percent and loan amounts is calculated with the aid of a financial calculator or computer software package. Thus, you will not have to compute the monthly payments necessary to amortize (retire) a loan over a period of time. However, you need to know (1) how to add property tax and hazard insurance costs to monthly mortgage payments to determine the total monthly payment to be paid to a lender, and (2) how to allocate correct portions of the monthly payment to interest and to payment on borrowed principal.

Adding Taxes and Insurance to Monthly Payment

One procedure for dealing with property taxes and hazard insurance is to begin with the level monthly mortgage payment (principal and interest) obtained from a loan table. To this amount are added $\frac{1}{12}$ of annual property taxes and $\frac{1}{12}$ of the annual hazard insurance premium. Together, these four items are referred to as a PITI payment (principal, interest, taxes, and insurance).

Example: A couple makes a monthly mortgage payment of $319.27 for principal and interest. Their annual property taxes are $784.20 and their homeowner's insurance is $192 per year. What is their total monthly PITI payment?

$$\$784.20 \div 12 \text{ months} = \$65.35 \text{ per month for taxes}$$
$$\$192 \div 12 \text{ months} = \$16.00 \text{ per month for insurance}$$
$$\text{Total monthly payment} = \$319.27 + \$65.35 + \$16$$
$$= \$400.62$$

PRACTICE PROBLEMS

30. A homeowner makes a monthly mortgage payment of $420.20 for principal and interest. Property taxes are $840 per year, and annual hazard insurance is $180. What is the total monthly PITI payment?

LOAN-TO-VALUE RATIO

The *loan-to-value ratio* (LTV or L/V) is the relationship between the amount borrowed and the appraised value (or purchase price) of a property. In other words, the L/V indicates what percent of the purchase price (or appraised value) the lender is willing to loan the borrower. It is a measure of the financial risk associated with lending and borrowing money.

FORMULA

Loan-to-Value Ratio

Loan amount ÷ Property value or Purchase price = Loan-to-value ratio

Example: A homeowner has a home worth $350,000 with a mortgage debt of $297,500. What is the loan-to-value ratio?

$297,500 loan amount ÷ $350,000 value = .85 or 85% loan-to-value ratio

Example: A borrower purchases a home and is required to make a down payment of $25,000. The loan-to-value ratio is 75 percent. What is the amount of the loan?

Use the T-device to solve this problem. The $25,000 down payment is the *part*. The *rate* is the percent that represents the down payment *not* the loan amount.

100% – 75% loan = 25% down payment

So the $25,000 down payment represents 25 percent of the purchase price. $25,000 down payment ÷ .25 rate = $100,000 purchase price
The amount of the loan is the purchase price (or total value) minus the down payment:

$100,000 value – $25,000 down payment = $75,000 loan

PRACTICE PROBLEMS

31. A buyer obtains an 80 percent loan on a $90,000 purchase price. What is the loan amount?

Mortgage Math **79**

ADVANCED MORTGAGE PROBLEMS

Alas, the solution to one or two math problems you encounter on your license exam may not seem readily apparent. In the following example, you are asked to calculate the sale price. What makes this problem tricky is figuring out what to plug in for the *rate*.

Example: A transaction closes with an existing mortgage of $45,800, cash to the seller of $10,600. Closing costs are 6 percent of the sale price. What is the sale price?

If we add the existing mortgage pay off and the cash to the seller at closing, we have the total net proceeds after paying closing costs:

$45,800 mortgage + $10,600 cash to seller = $56,400

The $56,400 is net after closing costs, so we can use 100% − 6% = 94% for our *rate*:

$56,400 ÷ .94 = $60,000 purchase price

MORTGAGE AMORTIZATION

Mortgages usually call for regular, equal payments (level-payment plan) that include both interest payments and payments on the unpaid balance of the debt (principal). The amount of the payment that goes for interest gradually decreases, and the amount assigned to amortizing the debt (principal) gradually increases over the life of the mortgage. Webster defines the word *amortize* as meaning to extinguish or deaden. An **amortized mortgage** is gradually and systematically killed or extinguished by regular periodic payments.

To calculate how much money is to be regarded as interest and how much is to be paid on the principal, three facts are needed:

1. The outstanding amount of the debt (principal)

2. The rate of interest

3. The amount of the payment per period (usually monthly)

The easiest way to solve amortized mortgage problems is to use a systematic approach. The following procedure is easy to use and will reduce the chance of error. When calculating the amortization of a mortgage, sketch the following column headings on a piece of paper:

	Interest	Principal Reduction	New Principal Balance
First month			
Second month			
Third month (and so on)			

By using this format, the required steps to solve an amortization problem become apparent. The first month's interest is the initial entry in the table. Once the first month's interest has been computed and entered, the next two column headings, *Principal Reduction* and *New Principal Balance*, indicate the next pieces of information needed.

Before going through an example, it is important to note the relationship of the following three steps for amortizing mortgages to the above format:

Amortizing a Mortgage

Step 1   Principal balance × Annual interest rate ÷ 12 = First month's interest (place under *Interest* in table)

Step 2   Monthly mortgage payment – First month's interest = Payment on principal (place under *Principal Reduction*)

Step 3   Beginning principal balance – Principal payment = New principal balance (place under *New Principal Balance*)

Repeat the above steps as many times as are required.

Example: You sell a home with a mortgage of $45,000 at 9½ percent interest. The prospect wants you to explain how much of her monthly payment is interest and how much is applied to the principal during the first three months. Her monthly payment is $378.38.

Step 1 $45,000 × .095 ÷ 12 = $356.25 first month's interest
(enter under *Interest*)

Step 2 $378.38 – 356.25 = $22.13 payment on principal
(enter under *Principal Reduction*)

To continue with month two, take credit for the $22.13 paid on the principal by subtracting that amount from the $45,000 beginning mortgage.

Step 3 $45,000.00 – 22.13 = $44,977.87 unpaid principal balance
(enter under *New Principal Balance*)

Repeat these steps for the second and third months.

Step 1 $44,977.87 × .095 ÷ 12 = $356.0748 second month's interest
(round to $356.07 and enter under *Interest*)

Step 2 $378.38 – 356.07 = $22.31 second month's principal
(enter under *Principal Reduction*)

Step 3 $44,977.87 – 22.31 = $44,955.56 new principal balance
(enter under *New Principal Balance*)

Step 1 $44,955.56 × .095 ÷ 12 = $355.8982 third month's interest
(round to $355.90 and enter under *Interest*)

Step 2 $378.38 – 355.90 = $22.48 third month's principal (enter under *Principal Reduction*)

Thus, the answer to your prospect's question is:

	Interest	Principal
First month:	$356.25	$22.13
Second month:	$356.07	$22.31
Third month:	$355.90	$22.48

32. Mr. and Mrs. Lovejoy have obtained a mortgage loan of $75,000 at 9¼ percent interest. The loan will be amortized by equal monthly payments of $617.01 over a period of 30 years. The monthly payment includes both principal and interest. What portion of the third month's payment will be applied to principal?

Working With Loan Constants

A loan constant or mortgage constant is the percentage of the original amount borrowed required to be repaid each year in order to pay the annual interest on the outstanding balance and fully amortize (pay off) the loan over the term of the loan. A monthly loan constant is the percentage of the original amount borrowed that must be paid each month to pay off the principal and interest over the term of the loan.

Example: A borrower obtained a loan in the amount of $58,600 at 6 percent interest per annum with 360 monthly payments of $351.34 principal and interest. What is the monthly loan constant?

To solve this problem, use the T-device. The loan amount is the *total* and the monthly payment is the *part*. We need to solve for the loan constant, which is the *rate*.

$351.34 (part) ÷ $58,600 (total) = .0059956 (rate)

Now let's solve a word problem that states the amount of the loan constant.

Example: A house sells for $130,000. The interest rate is 7 percent with a 10 percent down payment. The loan constant is .006653. Calculate the interest for month three.

At first glance we see that we are asked for the interest payment in month three. So we are calculating a mortgage amortization. But something is different this time. We don't know the monthly P&I payment. Instead we have been given the loan constant.

Also notice that we have not been given the loan amount. Let's solve for the loan amount first. The borrower is putting down 10 percent. So the amount of the loan is 90 percent of the sale price:

$130,000 × .90 = $117,000

Ok. Now we use our trusty T-device to solve for the monthly P&I payment. The loan amount is the *total* and the loan constant is the *rate*:

$117,000 × .006653 = $778.40 monthly mortgage payment

Now, it's a straightforward amortization problem! Go ahead and amortize the loan for 3 months and compare your figures to the chart below:

	Interest	Principal
First month:	$682.50	$95.90
Second month:	$681.94	$96.46
Third month:	$681.38	$97.02

Amortization Over Extended Periods

It may become necessary to calculate the amount of interest paid over an extended period of time. For example, suppose a customer has been making a monthly payment on her mortgage for 14 years and is informed by the mortgagee (lender) that 22 percent of the mortgage has been paid. She asks you to calculate the total amount of interest she has paid on the loan during the 14 years she has been making payments.

You know that payments have been made for 14 years. You also know that 168 payments have been made (12 months × 14 years = 168 monthly payments). Multiply the total number of monthly payments made by the amount of the monthly payment required in the mortgage agreement to determine the total amount paid during the 14-year period. From this total amount paid, subtract the amount that has been paid on the mortgage (22 percent of the original loan amount). The difference is interest.

Example: You have paid $465.12 on your mortgage each month for 10 years. You learn that your mortgage is 17 percent paid off after 10 years. If the original amount borrowed was $53,900, how much total interest have you paid to date?

Step 1

$$
\begin{array}{r}
12 = \text{months in a year} \\
\underline{\times\ 10} = \text{years paid on mortgage} \\
120 = \text{months paid on mortgage to date}
\end{array}
$$

Step 2

$$
\begin{array}{r}
\$\quad 465.12 = \text{monthly mortgage payment} \\
\underline{\times\ 120} = \text{months paid on mortgage to date} \\
\$55,814.40 = \text{total amount paid to date}
\end{array}
$$

Step 3

$$
\begin{array}{r}
\$\ \ 53,900 = \text{amount originally borrowed} \\
\underline{\times\ .17} = \text{percent of loan repaid to date} \\
\$9,163.00 = \text{principal repaid on loan to date}
\end{array}
$$

Step 4

$$
\begin{array}{r}
\$55,814.40 = \text{total amount paid to date} \\
\underline{-\ 9,163.00} = \text{principal repaid on loan to date} \\
\$46,651.40 = \text{total interest paid to date}
\end{array}
$$

Example: Assume that you pay on the mortgage in the previous example throughout the entire 30-year period and pay it off completely. How much additional interest will be paid during the last 20 years of the mortgage?

Step 1

$$
\begin{array}{r}
12 = \text{months in a year} \\
\underline{\times\ 30} = \text{years paid on mortgage} \\
360 = \text{months paid on mortgage}
\end{array}
$$

Step 2

$$
\begin{array}{r}
\$465.12 = \text{monthly mortgage payment} \\
\underline{\times\ 360} = \text{months paid on mortgage} \\
\$167,443.20 = \text{total amount paid}
\end{array}
$$

Step 3 $167,443.20 = total amount paid
$\underline{-\ 53,900.00}$ = amount originally borrowed
$113,543.20 = total interest paid

The question, however, asks how much additional interest was paid during the last 20 years.

Step 4 $113,543.20 = total interest paid
$\underline{-\ 46,651.40}$ = interest paid over the first 10 years
$\ 66,891.80 = additional interest paid during the last 20 years

---

33. Mrs. South is thinking of selling her home. She obtains the following information from the bank financing her home. Over a period of 9 years, Mrs. South has paid off 12 percent of her mortgage. The original mortgage was $42,000 at 11 percent for 30 years. Her monthly payments for principal and interest have been $399.98 per month. How much interest has Mrs. South paid on her mortgage during the 9 years?

34. The monthly mortgage payments are $320.50 and have been paid for 10 years. If the original loan amount was $30,000 and after 10 years is 69 percent paid off, what is the total interest paid to date?

35. Mary Carson borrows $40,000 for 30 years at 10 percent. She pays a total of $86,370.80 in interest during the term of the loan. How much was the monthly mortgage payment?

ANSWER KEY

1. Rate = interest ÷ (principal × time);
    $146.25 interest ÷ ($3,000 principal × 6 months);
    $146.25 ÷ ($3,000 × .5);
    $146.25 ÷ $1,500 = .0975 or 9.75%

2. Interest = principal × rate × time;
    $68,000 principal × .116 rate × .75 time = $5,916

3. Time = interest ÷ (principal × rate);
    $60 interest ÷ ($2,000 principal × .09 rate);
    $60 ÷ $180 = .333 or 4 months

4. Principal = interest ÷ rate;
    $900 × 2 = $1,800 interest;
    $1,800 ÷ .06 = $30,000 principal

5. $58,800 (*total*) ÷ .80 (*rate*) = $73,500 (*part*)
    appraised value;
    $73,500 × .10 = $7,350 in escrow

6. $79,500 sale price × .75 = $59,625 loan amount;
    $79,500 – $59,625 = $19,875 down payment;
    $19,875 – $5,000 earnest money =
    $14,875 remaining down payment

7. $89,700 purchase price × .90 loan =
    $80,730 mortgage amount;
    $89,700 – $80,730 = $8,970 down payment

8. $71,500 sale price × .90 = $64,350 loan amount;
    $64,350 × .015 = $965.25 (PMI);
    $71,500 – $64,350 = $7,150 down payment;
    $7,150 – $1,000 deposit =
    $6,150 unpaid down payment;
    $6,150 + $965.25 = $7,115.25 total due at closing

9. $69,700 sale price × .95 financing = $66,215 loan

10. $44,500 sale price or appraised value × .9875 =
    $43,943.75 rounded to $43,944 maximum FHA
    loan amount;
    $44,500 × .03 = $1,335 minimum cash investment

11. $72,400 sale price/appraised value × .9775 =
    $70,771 maximum FHA loan amount;
    $72,400 × .03 = $2,172 minimum cash investment

12. $92,000 sale price/appraised value × .9775 =
    $89,930 maximum FHA loan amount;
    $92,000 × .03 = $2,760 minimum cash investment

13. $44,500 sale price + $800 closing costs =
    $45,300 total acquisition cost;
    $45,300 – $43,944 maximum FHA loan amount =
    $1,356; $1,356 is equal to or greater than the mini-
    mum cash investment of $1,335 therefore the loan
    amount does not need to be adjusted (However, if
    the problem indicated to round the FHA loan to an
    even $50 increment, the loan would be reduced to
    $43,900 and the $44 would be added to the down
    payment.)

14. $72,400 sale price + $500 closing costs =
    $72,900 total acquisition cost;
    $72,900 – $70,771 maximum FHA loan amount =
    $2,129; $2,129 is less than the required minimum
    cash investment so the loan amount must be
    reduced by the difference:
    $2,172 minimum cash investment – $2,129
    calculated down payment = $43 difference;
    The loan amount must be reduced by the $43 to
    meet the required minimum investment

15. $92,000 sale price + $1,000 closing costs =
    $93,000 total acquisition cost;
    $93,000 – $89,930 maximum FHA loan amount =
    $3,070 calculated down payment
    $3,070 is greater than or equal to the minimum
    cash investment of $2,760 therefore the loan
    amount does not need to be adjusted (However, if
    the problem indicated to round the FHA loan to an
    even $50 increment, the loan would be reduced to
    $89,900 and the $30 would be added to the down
    payment.)

16. $87,900 loan amount × .02 = $1,758

17. 6½% + (2 × ⅛%);
    6⅜ + ⅜ = 6⅝ = 6¾% yield

18. $77,500 sale price × .9775 =
    $75,756 maximum FHA loan;
    $77,500 × .03 = $2,325 required investment;
    $77,500 – $75,756 = $1,744;
    The required investment has not been met so the
    loan must be reduced to
    $77,500 – $2,325 = $75,175;
    $75,175 × .04 = $3,007 discount points

19. 4 points = $4 \times \frac{1}{8}\% = \frac{4}{8}\% = \frac{1}{2}\%$;
    $7\% + \frac{1}{2}\% = 7\frac{1}{2}\%$ real yield

20. $8.25\% - 7.5\% = .75\%$;
    $.75\% \div .125\% = 6$ points

21. $\$63,000 \times .04 = \$2,520$ price increase

22. Going at 95 means that 5 discount points are
    charged; $5 \times \frac{1}{8} = \frac{5}{8}$;
    $6\frac{1}{2} = 6\frac{4}{8} + \frac{5}{8} = 6\frac{9}{8} = 7\frac{1}{8}$ APR

23. $\$125,000 \times .80 = \$100,000$ loan amount;
    $\$100,000 \times .02 = \$2,000$ discount points

24. $\$1,245$ PITI $\div \$3,300$ monthly income =
    .377 or 38%
    No, 38% exceeds the monthly housing expense
    limit of 28%

25. $\$48,000 \times .002 = \$96$ intangible tax;
    $\$48,000 \div \$100$ increments $\times \$.35 =$
    $\$168$ doc stamps on note

26. $\$87,000 \times .002 = \$174$ intangible tax;
    $\$87,000 \div \$100$ increments $\times \$.35 =$
    $\$304.50$ doc stamps on note

27. $\$56,850 \times .002 = \$113.70$ intangible tax;
    $\$56,850 \div \$100$ increments =
    568.5, rounded to 569;
    569 taxable increments $\times \$.35 =$
    $\$199.15$ doc stamps on note

28. $\$92,760 \times .002 = \$185.52$ intangible tax;
    $\$92,760 \div \$100$ increments =
    927.6, rounded to 928;
    928 taxable increments $\times \$.35 =$
    $\$324.80$ doc stamps on note

29. $\$126,420 \times .002 = \$252.84$ intangible tax;
    $\$126,420 \div \$100$ increments =
    1,264.2, rounded to 1,265;
    1,265 taxable increments $\times \$.35 =$
    $\$442.75$ doc stamps on note

30. $\$840 \div 12$ months = $\$70$ per month for taxes;
    $\$180 \div 12$ months = $\$15$ per month for insurance;
    $\$420.20 + \$70 + \$15 = \$505.20$ total monthly
    payment (PITI)

31. $\$90,000$ purchase price $\times .80 =$
    $\$72,000$ loan amount

32. $\$75,000 \times .0925 \div 12$ months =
    $\$578.13$ interest month one; $\$617.01 - \$578.13 =$
    $\$38.88$ principal paid, month one;
    $\$75,000 - \$38.88 = \$74,961.12$ unpaid principal
    balance; $\$74,961.12 \times .0925 \div 12$ months =
    $\$577.83$ interest month two;
    $\$617.01 - \$577.83 =$
    $\$39.18$ principal paid, month two;
    $\$74,961.12 - \$39.18 =$
    $\$74,921.94$ unpaid principal balance;
    $\$74,921.94 \times .0925 \div 12$ months =
    $\$577.52$ interest month three;
    $\$617.01 - \$577.52 =$
    $\$39.49$ principal paid, month three

33. 12 months $\times$ 9 years = 108 monthly payments;
    $\$399.98 \times 108 = \$43,197.84$ paid to date;
    $\$42,000$ loan $\times .12 = \$5,040$ principal paid to date;
    $\$43,197.84 - \$5,040 =$
    $\$38,157.84$ interest paid to date

34. $\$320.50 \times 12 \times 10$ years = $\$38,460$ paid to date;
    $\$30,000 \times .69 = \$20,700$ principal paid;
    $\$38,460 - \$20,700 = \$17,760$ interest paid to date

35. $\$86,370.80$ total interest + $\$40,000$ total principal =
    $\$126,370.80$ paid in full;
    30 years $\times$ 12 = 360 monthly payments;
    $\$126,370.80 \div 360 = \$351.03$ monthly payments

Chapter Six

REAL ESTATE TAXES

KEY TERMS

Ad Valorem Tax a tax based on the value of the item being taxed

Assessed Valuation the value established for property tax purposes

Homestead Exemption a reduction in the assessed value allowed for one's principal residence

Mill one one-thousandth of a dollar and one tenth of a cent; used in expressing tax rates on a per-dollar basis

Special Assessment a tax levied against property to pay for all or part of an improvement that will benefit the property being assessed

Taxable Value the assessed value less allowable exemptions; an amount to which the tax rate is applied to determine property taxes due

Overview

Property taxes provide much of the revenue needed by local governments to fund public services. Property taxes are most commonly levied on an **ad valorem** basis, or according to the value of the property.

The county property appraiser is charged with assessing a fair and reasonable value for all property. Property appraisers apply the three approaches to value: sales comparison, cost depreciation, and income. **Assessed value** is the value of a property established for property tax purposes.

TAXABLE VALUE

Taxable value (nonexempt assessed value) is determined by subtracting any applicable tax exemptions from the assessed value of the property.

Example: A home is assessed at $70,000. The owners have qualified for the homestead tax exemption. Assuming a **homestead exemption** of $25,000, what is the taxable value of this home?

FORMULA

Taxable Value

Assessed value – Homestead exemption = Taxable value

$$\$70,000 - \$25,000 = \$45,000$$

PRACTICE PROBLEMS

1. Using the taxable value formula, what is the taxable value of a property that is assessed at $318,000 if the homeowners qualify for a homestead tax exemption of $25,000?

_____

The taxable value is the amount to which the appropriate *tax rate* is applied to determine the amount of property taxes to be paid. This tax rate is usually expressed in mills rather than in decimal form. A **mill** is one one-thousandth of a dollar. There are 1,000 mills in a dollar. Thus, a tax rate of .010 can be expressed as 10 mills per dollar.

To convert the tax rate from a decimal form to mills, simply move the decimal point three places to the *right*. Add zeros, if necessary. For example, .035 can be written as 35 mills. Moving the decimal place three places to the right is the same as multiplying the decimal by 1,000.

To convert millage to the decimal form, place the decimal point three places to the *left* of the written (or unwritten) decimal point. For example, 9 mills = .009 and 26.8 mills = .0268. This is the same as dividing the mills by 1,000.

> **Hint:** When expressing mills in decimal form, always use three digits to avoid possible confusion. For example, write 20 mills in decimal form as .020.

Tax rates may be expressed in many ways. For instance, the tax rate of .021 may also be expressed as:

21 mills per $1 of assessed valuation

$.021 per $1 of assessed valuation

$2.10 per $100 of assessed valuation

$21 per $1,000 of assessed valuation

Each of the four statements above is a different way of expressing the same quantity.

PRACTICE PROBLEMS

Convert these mills to decimals.

2. 1 mill = _____

3. 10 mills = _____

4. 100 mills = _____

Convert these decimal numbers to mills.

5. .016589 = _____

6. .003014 = _____

7. .03554 = _____

CITY AND COUNTY PROPERTY TAXES

Remember the earlier example in which a home was assessed at $70,000 and the homeowners qualified for a homestead tax exemption of $25,000? Let's use that example to calculate the property taxes. Assume that the tax rate is 16 mills. The calculation is as follows:

$70,000 – $25,000 = $45,000 taxable value

$45,000 × .016 (the property tax rate) = $720

The tax rate is always applied to the taxable value. If no exemptions apply, the taxable value and the assessed value are the same. However, if any exemptions do apply, they must be deducted from the assessed value to determine the taxable value. To find the dollar amount of property taxes, always multiply the taxable value by the tax rate.

FORMULA

Taxable Value

Assessed value – Tax exemption(s) = Taxable value

Taxes Owed

Taxable value × Tax rate = Dollar amount of taxes

Example: Mr. Pasco owns a home in the city. The city tax rate is 8.7 mills, the county tax rate is 9.2 mills and the school board tax rate is 8 mills. Mr. Pasco has qualified for a homestead tax exemption of $25,000. His home has been assessed at $64,500. What must Mr. Pasco pay in property taxes?

$64,500 − 25,000 = $39,500 taxable value

8.7 + 9.2 + 8.0 = 25.9 mills

$39,500 × .0259 (or 25.9 mills) = $1,023.05

Example: If Mr. Pasco is interested in finding the amount of savings in property taxes realized by the exemption:

FORMULA

Tax Savings

Exemption × Tax rate = Tax savings

$25,000 × .0259 = $647.50

Example: What if Mr. Pasco lived outside the city limits in the same county? How much difference, if any, would there be in his property taxes? Mr. Pasco would still be charged for county and school board taxes. However, he would not be charged for city taxes. The solution is exactly the same as above, with one exception: subtract the city tax rate of 8.7 mills from the former total of 25.9 mills, leaving a new effective tax rate of 17.2 mills (.0172). Alternatively, simply add 9.2 county mills + 8.0 school board mills = 17.2 mills.

$64,500 − $25,000 = $39,500 taxable value

$39,500 × .0172 = $679.40

The difference is $343.65 ($1,023.05 − $679.40 = $343.65, or $39,500 × 8.7 mills = $39,500 × .0087 = $343.65).

PRACTICE PROBLEMS

Use the following information to answer problems 8 through 11:

The city tax rate is 9 mills, the county rate is 8.5 mills, and the school board rate is 6 mills. The property is homesteaded. The assessed value is $285,000.

8. Calculate the total millage rate. _____

9. What is the taxable value of the property? _____

10. How much does the owner owe in property taxes? _____

11. How much did the $25,000 homestead exemption save the homeowner in property taxes?

_____

ADDITIONAL EXEMPTIONS FROM PROPERTY TAXES

Up to this point, we have discussed applying a base $25,000 tax exemption on homesteaded property. Many states provide for additional special exemptions for persons with disabilities or because of age and so forth. For example, a chart of special exemptions applicable to homesteaded property in Florida is shown on the following page. Check with your instructor regarding applicable exemptions in your state.

Special Tax Exemptions on Homesteaded Property in Florida	
$500	Widows and widowers (a surviving spouse who has not remarried)
$500	Legally blind persons
$500	Totally and permanently disabled nonveterans
$5,000	Disabled veterans who are at least 10 percent disabled from military service-connected misfortune

Example: Assume that a Florida homeowner is a widow and is legally blind. The property has an assessed value of $122,000 and is homesteaded. If the millage rate is 30 mills, how much does the homeowner owe in property taxes?

To calculate the applicable total homestead exemptions, add the special exemptions to the base homestead exemption of $25,000:

$25,000 + $500 widow exemption + $500 blind exemption =

$26,000 total applicable homestead exemption

$122,000 assessed value – $26,000 applicable exemptions = $96,000 taxable value

$96,000 taxable value × .030 = $2,880

PRACTICE PROBLEMS

12. A Floridian is a veteran of the Iraq War who is 25 percent disabled from injuries suffered in the war. The veteran's residence is homesteaded and has an assessed value of $230,000. What is the taxable value of the veteran's homesteaded property?

USING THE T-DEVICE IN PROPERTY TAX PROBLEMS

Remember the T-device we used in Chapter 3? You will be pleased to know that the T-device can be used to solve real estate property tax problems!

Taxable Value = *total*

Tax rate = *rate*

Amount of taxes = *part*

$$\frac{\text{Taxes}}{\text{Taxable} \times \text{Tax}}$$
$$\frac{}{\text{value} \quad | \quad \text{rate}}$$

Example: Find the tax rate if Mr. Pasco paid $980.52 last year in property taxes on property assessed at $86,500. Assume that Mr. Pasco still qualified for the $25,000 homestead tax exemption.

$86,500 – $25,000 = $61,500 taxable value

$980.52 (*part*) ÷ $61,500 (*total*) = .01594 or 15.94 mills (*rate*)

$$\frac{\$980.52}{\$61,500 \times \quad ?}$$

In some states the assessed value of a property is a percentage of the market value. The T-device can be applied to determine the assessed value. Use market value as the *total*, and use the percent of market value that represents the assessed value for the *rate*.

$$\text{Market value} = total$$
$$\text{Percent of market value} = rate$$
$$\text{Assessed value} = part$$

$$\frac{\text{Assessed value}}{\text{Market value} \;\times\; \text{Percent of market value}}$$

Example: Assume that the assessed value of a house is 80 percent of full market value. If the market value is $92,000, what is the assessed value?

$$\$92{,}000\ (total) \times .80\ (rate) = \$73{,}600\ (part)$$

$$\frac{?}{\$92{,}000 \;\times\; 80\%}$$

CALCULATING THE MILLAGE RATE FOR A COMMUNITY

You may be asked on your license exam to determine the total mills needed to meet the budgetary requirements of a particular community. Let's begin by briefly discussing how a community determines the number of mills it must charge to meet the cost of operation. A local community begins by developing a budget that consists of all the expenses associated with operation. Expenses include such things as emergency medical services, police and fire protection, and so forth.

Local government depends on property taxes to meet much of its revenue needs. However, local government also receives revenue from sources including sales tax, building permits, speeding tickets, and other charges. If we take the total amount of revenue required by a local government (its budget) and subtract the revenue from sources other than property taxes (the nonproperty revenue) we can determine the amount of the budget that must be met from property taxes:

Total budget – Nonproperty revenue =
Revenue needed from property taxes

Ok. So far so good. But how do we get from the dollar amount of revenue we need from property taxes to the millage rate that must be charged to meet the budgetary needs? Remember how we calculated all of those homestead exemptions? Applicable homestead exemptions reduced the amount of property taxes that were charged. Somehow we have to take this into consideration when calculating the millage rate. We know that assessed value is used as a basis for property taxation but we subtracted applicable homestead exemptions to calculate the taxable value of property. We can use the same approach to calculate the amount of revenue available from all of the properties within a community.

Total assessed value – Applicable exemptions = Total taxable value

If you recall, only homesteaded properties were eligible for the special exemptions. However, government buildings and buildings owned by churches and nonprofit organizations are also exempt from property taxes. Therefore, the applicable exemptions include all of the property tax revenue not collected because of government exemptions, homestead exemptions, and so forth.

Perhaps applying what we have developed to this point will be clearer if we work through an example together.

Example: Assume that Duval County has an approved operating budget for the next fiscal year with expenditures of $27,500,000. A review of past and present experience indicates that revenue of $10,750,000 can be expected from sources other than real property revenue. The county property appraiser reports total assessed valuation of $750,000,000. Applicable exemptions total $125,000,000. What is the tax rate in mills that must be collected in order to meet the budgetary needs of this county?

And you thought sticking to your budget was tough! Ok, we can handle this rather cumbersome problem by taking one step at a time. Let's begin with figuring out how much revenue will be needed from property taxes:

Total budget − nonproperty revenue = revenue needed from property taxes

$$\$27,500,000 - \$10,750,000 = \$16,750,000$$

We know the total assessed valuation for the community. Our next step is to determine how much the taxable value is for all of the property within the community.

Total assessed value − applicable exemptions = total taxable value

$$\$750,000,000 - \$125,000,000 = \$625,000,000$$

Ok. But we need to know what the millage rate is. No problem! If we divide the revenue needed from property taxes by the total taxable value of the property within the community, it will indicate the millage rate we need to charge:

Revenue needed from property taxes ÷ total taxable value = millage rate

---

Hint: Cancel out the last three zeroes in the numerator and the denominator before plugging the numbers into your calculator. This is because a typical handheld calculator will only allow you to input eight digits. Canceling the last three digits in both numbers makes the calculation much easier to perform.

$$\$16,750,000 \div \$625,000,000 = \$16,750 \div \$625,000 = .0268 \text{ or } 26.8 \text{ mills}$$

PRACTICE PROBLEMS

13. The proposed budget is $20,000,000. Revenue from sources other than real estate totals $7,500,000. Total assessed value of real property in the community totals $700,000,000 and total applicable exemptions are $120,000,000. Calculate the tax rate for the community.

SPECIAL ASSESSMENTS

Special assessments are a one-time tax levied on properties to help pay for certain types of improvements to property.

Example: You live on an unpaved street. The city is petitioned to pave the street and agrees to do so. The paving cost is $24 per foot of frontage, and the city is to pay 30 percent of the cost. If your lot frontage on the street is 100 feet, what will be your special assessment for street paving?

> **Hint:** For exam purposes don't forget that the street has two sides, and the property across the street must bear its fair share.

100 front feet × $24 per foot of frontage = $2,400

$2,400 × .70 (owners' share of cost is 100% – 30%) = $1,680

$1,680 ÷ 2 (one half of street paving cost) = $840

PRACTICE PROBLEMS

14. High Springs is assessing all property owners on the streets affected for the cost of paving the streets. Property owners will have to pay 65 percent of the $25 cost per foot of frontage. Calculate the special paving assessment for a parcel of land with a frontage of 90 feet.

15. Clarkson City has agreed to pay 22 percent of the cost for installing sewer lines in a new subdivision. What will each property owner be required to pay as a special assessment if lots are a standard 100 feet of frontage and the cost of installation is $34 per foot of frontage?

16. The city is going to pave the streets in your neighborhood at a cost of $50 per foot of frontage and has agreed to pay 45 percent of the cost. Your property measures 136' × 150'. What will the special assessment cost you?

REAL PROPERTY TRANSFER TAXES

Most states tax the transfer of real estate. However, the tax rate and the considerations that are exempt from taxation differ from state to state. The procedures employed for solving problems related to transfer taxes are generally the same, whether the taxes are called *revenue stamp taxes, transfer taxes,* or *documentary stamp taxes.*

The types of real estate transfer taxes that may be levied on real property are discussed in the next section of this chapter.

State Documentary Stamp Tax on Deeds

The word *documentary* stems from the intent to imprint or place tax stamps on "documents" such as deeds. In some states, for example, the tax is $.70 for each $100 of the full purchase price (or fraction of $100). No exemptions are allowed.

Example: A farm sells for $115,500. The buyer pays an earnest money deposit of $15,000 and assumes an existing mortgage of $75,000. The seller takes back a second mortgage from the buyer for the balance of the purchase price. Using the cited rate of $.70 for each $100 of the full purchase price, how much will the seller need to pay for the state transfer tax on the deed?

State documentary stamp tax on deed:

$115,500 ÷ $100 = 1,155 taxable increments

1,155 × $.70 = $808.50 documentary stamp tax on deed

Example: A house sold for $86,000. The buyer paid $10,000 down and agreed to pay the balance in cash at closing. Using the previously cited rate, how much will the seller pay for the state transfer tax?

State documentary stamp tax on deed:

$86,000 ÷ $100 = 860 taxable increments

860 × $.70 = $602 documentary stamp tax on deed

> **Hint:** State documentary stamp tax on deeds is based on the entire purchase price of a property. The calculation does not take into consideration how the purchase price is paid (cash, assumption of mortgage or new mortgage).

The law in most states requires payment of a full increment of tax for any fractional portion of a taxable increment. Therefore, any fractional part must be rounded up to the next whole taxable increment.

Example: To illustrate, what would have been the cost of the state tax on the deed if the sale price of $115,500 in the first example had been $115,525 instead?

$115,525 ÷ $100 = 1,155.25 taxable increments

1,155.25 rounds up to 1,156 increments

1,156 × $.70 = $809.20 ($.70, or one additional increment)

Example: Calculate the cost of the state tax on the deed assuming a sale price of $115,450 and compare the result to the earlier example with a sale price of $115,500.

$115,450 ÷ $100 = 1,154.5 taxable increments

1,154.5 rounds up to 1,155 increments

1,155 × $.70 = $808.50 (no change)

It is also useful to practice with problems that include the need to calculate the two state taxes associated with financing (Chapter 5).

Use the following tax rates for the next five problems:

Intangible tax on mortgage	$.002 per dollar of face value
Documentary tax on note	$.35 per $100, or fraction of $100
Documentary tax on deed	$.70 per $100, or fraction of $100

17.

Sale price	$72,800
FHA mortgage assumed	$59,780
New second mortgage taken back by seller	$12,020
Cash from buyer	$ 1,000

State documentary stamp tax on deed _____

18. Sale price (Buyer paid all cash) $66,950

State documentary stamp tax on deed _____

Compute all of the appropriate state taxes in practice problems 19 through 21 using the following information:

Sale price	$73,000
Existing mortgage assumed	$57,825
Second mortgage to seller	$10,100
Cash paid by buyer	$ 5,075

19. State documentary stamp tax on deed _____

20. State documentary stamp tax on the notes associated with the mortgages in this transaction

_____

21. Intangible tax on new mortgage _____

Compute the appropriate state taxes in practice problems 22 through 24 using the following information:

Sale price	$89,750
Existing mortgage (paid off at closing)	$18,900
New mortgage by buyer	$71,800
Cash paid by buyer	$17,950

22. State documentary stamp tax on deed _____

23. State documentary stamp tax on note _____

24. Intangible tax on new mortgage _____

25. A property sells for $185,000 with the buyer assuming the existing first mortgage of $112,530 and the seller taking back a purchase money mortgage in the amount of $32,000. What are the total taxes due on this transaction?

_____

ANSWER KEY

1. $318,000 assessed value – $25,000 exemption = $293,000 taxable value

2. 1 mill = .001

3. 10 mills = .010

4. 100 mills = .100

5. .016589 = 16.589 mills

6. .003014 = 3.014 mills

7. .03554 = 35.54 mills

8. 9.0 + 8.5 + 6.0 = 23.5 mills or .0235

9. $285,000 assessed value – $25,000 homestead = $260,000

10. $260,000 taxable value × .0235 = $6,110

11. $25,000 exemption × .0235 = $587.50 tax savings

12. $25,000 homestead exemption + $5,000 military exemption =
$30,000 applicable homestead exemptions;
$230,000 – $30,000 exemptions =
$200,000 taxable value

13. Total budget – nonproperty revenue =
revenue needed from property taxes;
$20,000,000 – $7,500,000 = $12,500,000;
Total assessed value – applicable exemptions =
total taxable value;
$700,000,000 – $120,000,000 = $580,000,000;
Revenue needed from property taxes ÷ total
taxable value = millage rate;
(Delete last 3 digits in both numbers before
dividing); $12,500 ÷ 580,000 = .0215517 or
21.6 mills (rounded)

14. 90 feet of frontage × $25 =
$2,250 cost to pave 90 feet;
$2,250 × .65 = $1,462.50; $1,462.50 ÷ 2 =
$731.25 property owner's share

15. 100 feet of frontage × $34 =
$3,400 cost to install 100' of sewer;
$3,400 × (100% – 22%); $3,400 × .78 = $2,652;
$2,652 ÷ 2 = $1,326 owner's cost

16. 136 feet of frontage × $50 =
$6,800 total cost of assessment;
$6,800 × 55% homeowner's percent = $3,740;
$3,740 ÷ 2 = $1,870 homeowner's cost on one
side of the street

17. $72,800 ÷ $100 = 728 taxable increments;
728 × $.70 = $509.60

18. $66,950 ÷ $100 = 669.5 taxable increments;
669.5 rounds up to 670 increments;
670 × $.70 = $469

19. $73,000 ÷ $100 = 730 taxable increments;
730 × $.70 = $511

20. $10,100 ÷ $100 = 101 taxable increments;
101 × $.35 = $35.35 doc stamps on new note;
$57,825 ÷ $100 = 578.25 rounded up to 579
taxable increments;
579 × $.35 = $202.65 doc stamps on assumed
mortgage note;
$35.35 + $202.65 = $238 total doc stamps on
notes

21. $10,100 × $.002 = $20.20

22. $89,750 ÷ $100 = 897.50 taxable increments;
897.5 rounds up to 898 increments;
898 × $.70 = $628.60

23. $71,800 ÷ $100 = 718 taxable increments;
718 × $.35 = $251.30

24. $71,800 × $.002 = $143.60

25. Doc stamps on deed: $185,000 ÷ $100 increments =
1850 × $.70 = $1,295;
Doc stamps on assumed mortgage:
$112,530 ÷ $100 increments =
1,125.3 rounded up to 1,126 increments × $.35 =
$394.10;
Doc stamps on new mortgage:
$32,000 ÷ $100 increments = 320 × $.35 = $112;
Intangible tax on new mortgage: $32,000 × $.002 =
64; $1,295 + $394.10 + $112 + $64 = $1,865.10

Chapter Seven

APPRAISING AND INVESTING CALCULATIONS

KEY TERMS

Accrued Depreciation total depreciation that has accumulated over the years an improvement has been standing; the difference (loss) in value between an existing building and an exact replica in new condition

Actual Age the chronological age of a structure (*not* the effective age or economic life)

Capitalization Rate the rate divided into net operating income to obtain value

Comparable recently sold property similar to the one being appraised

Depreciation loss in value for any reason

Economic Life period of time a property may be expected to be profitable or productive; useful life

Effective Age age indicated by the condition and utility of a structure at the time of inspection

Effective Gross Income anticipated income from the operation of a property after adjusting for vacancy and collection losses

Market Value the most probable price a property should bring in a competitive market when there has been a normal exposure time, arm's-length bargaining, typical financing, and informed parties who are willing but not compelled to buy or sell

Net Operating Income revenue remaining after expenses have been deducted

Potential Gross Income maximum potential income, assuming the property is fully rented at market rates

Replacement Cost New the amount of money required to replace a structure having the same use and functional utility as the subject property, but using modern, available, or updated materials

Reproduction Cost New amount required to duplicate in exact detail the building being appraised

Subject Property property being appraised or evaluated

Vacancy and Collection deduction from potential gross income to allow for tenant turnover

Chapter | **Overview**

Estimating the value of real property is an important activity, as is analyzing financial and investment matters pertaining to income-producing properties. This chapter focuses on the basic arithmetic used in the appraisal field. The chapter also includes a discussion of arithmetic important to real estate investment decisions.

Most typically an appraiser is hired to estimate the market value of real property. **Market value** is defined as:

> the most probable price that a property should bring in a competitive and open market under all conditions requisite to a fair sale, assuming that the buyer and seller are both acting prudently and knowledgeably and that the price is not affected by undue stimulus.

There are three approaches to estimating the value of real property:

1. Cost approach

2. Sales comparison approach

3. Income capitalization approach

Let's begin with a discussion of the cost approach.

COST APPROACH

The cost approach (or the *cost-depreciation approach*) is based on the theory that a knowledgeable purchaser will pay no more for a property than the cost of acquiring a similar site and constructing an acceptable substitute structure. The maximum value of a property can be measured by determining the cost to acquire an equivalent site and to reproduce a structure as if new, then subtracting accrued depreciation. This process can be expressed mathematically as:

FORMULA

Cost Approach

Reproduction cost new of the building – Accrued depreciation + Site value = Indicated value of the property

Before we begin any math calculations, we need an understanding of the appraisal terms used in the cost approach. An appraiser typically begins by estimating the reproduction cost new of the structure being appraised. **Reproduction cost new** is the amount that would be required to *duplicate exactly* the building being appraised. However, sometimes an appraiser chooses to use replacement cost new rather than reproduction cost new. **Replacement cost new** is today's cost of improvements that would have the *same functional utility* as the building being appraised, but the cost would be based on using modern building materials and building techniques. Consider an historic Craftsman-style home. Reproduction cost new is the cost to duplicate the home in exact detail, including the hand-carved trim on the porch. However, because many of the materials and building techniques are no longer used, the appraiser may choose to estimate the replacement cost new of reconstructing the Craftsman-style home with modern materials and techniques that closely resemble the original materials.

Depreciation is the loss in value for any reason. Types of depreciation include physical deterioration, functional obsolescence, and external obsolescence.

An appraiser estimates the dollar value of depreciation and subtracts that amount from the reproduction cost new of the structure. **Accrued depreciation** is the total depreciation that has accumulated over the years a building has been standing. Accrued depreciation is the difference (loss) in value between an existing building and an exact replica in new condition.

Land value is estimated as if the site were vacant. Land is *not* depreciated in the cost-depreciation approach. Only the buildings or other improvements to land are subject to depreciation. When the cost to reproduce the improvements is determined, depreciation is applied only to that portion of the property.

Cost Approach: Estimating Reproduction Cost New

Reproduction cost new of a building is typically estimated on a square foot basis. Cost estimating publications are used to estimate cost per square foot for living area, garage area, and so forth, based on quality of construction and types of materials used in the property being appraised. (Refer to the chart below.) The appraiser measures outside dimensions of the structure to determine the square feet of the subject property for the various types of square feet, such as living area and garage space. The types of square footage are considered separately because the cost per square foot is much higher for heated and air-conditioned living area compared with garage square footage or a screened-in porch.

Example: Referring to a cost manual, the appraiser estimates the reproduction cost new of each type of square footage:

Reproduction Cost New

Main living area:	1,540 square feet × $75 per square foot	= $115,500
Utility room:	117 square feet × $30 per square foot	= $ 3,510
Entrance porch	75 square feet × $25 per square foot	= $ 1,875
Garage	448 square feet × $40 per square foot	= $ 17,920
	Total estimated reproduction cost new:	$138,805

PRACTICE PROBLEMS

1.   A home has a living area of 60' × 35' and an attached garage that is 22' × 25'. In today's market the cost to build the main living area of the house is $80 per square foot. The garage costs $42 per square foot. What is the home's reproduction cost new?

Cost Approach: Estimating Depreciation

The simplest way to estimate depreciation is the *straight-line method*. This method spreads the total depreciation over the estimated economic life of a building in equal annual amounts. This means that an equal amount of building value is lost each year until the economic life of the building is exhausted. **Economic life** is the total estimated time in years that a property can be profitably useful. The number of years of economic life for a building must be estimated.

Straight-line depreciation is estimated by dividing the dollar cost to reproduce the building new by the total years of useful life.

Annual Depreciation

Total cost to reproduce new ÷ Years of useful life = Annual depreciation

Example: The cost to reproduce a building new is $116,000. The total years of economic life is estimated at 40 years. Using the straight-line method, estimate the amount of annual depreciation.

Annual depreciation = $116,000 ÷ 40 years = $2,900

To find the amount of accrued depreciation, multiply the annual depreciation by the building's **actual age.**

Accrued Depreciation

Annual depreciation × Actual age of the building = Accrued depreciation

Example: Using the previous problem, calculate the accrued depreciation of the building, assuming an actual age of 8 years.

Accrued depreciation = $2,900 × 8 years = $23,200

Example: Assuming the estimated land value of the above property is $20,000, what is the estimated value?

Property Value Using Cost Approach

Building reproduction cost new − Accrued depreciation + Land value = Property value

$116,000 − $23,200 + $20,000 = $112,800 property value

2. Use the reproduction cost new calculated in problem 1. Calculate the annual depreciation assuming an economic life of 50 years.

   _____

3. Use the annual depreciation that you calculated in problem 2. What is the accrued depreciation using an actual age of six years?

   _____

4. Use the information that you calculated in problems 1 through 3. If the site value is $25,000, what is the estimated property value?

   _____

More often appraisers in actual practice use the age-life method to estimate depreciation. The *age-life method* is based on a ratio of a property's effective age to its economic life. This method is thought to be a better method because it takes into account the property's condition. A home may be five years old, however, if the structure has been maintained well, its effective age may be estimated to be just two years. Therefore, this method attempts to deduct depreciation based on the actual condition of the structure rather than strictly on a straight annual allowance.

Age-Life Accrued Depreciation

Effective age ÷ Total economic life = Age-life accrued depreciation

Example: Assume a structure is 10 years old and has an effective age of seven years. The appraiser estimates the total economic life at 50 years. If the reproduction cost new is $327,500, what is the accrued depreciation using the age-life method?

To calculate the accrued depreciation we take the reproduction cost new times the ratio of effective age divided by total economic life. Let's write this in a mathematical equation:

$$\$327,500 \times (7 \text{ effective age} \div 50 \text{ total economic life}) = \text{age-life accrued depreciation}$$

Begin by performing the operation within the parentheses:

$$7 \div 50 = .14, \text{ so:}$$

$$\$327,500 \times .14 = \text{age-life accrued depreciation}$$

$$\$327,500 \times .14 = \$45,850 \text{ age-life accrued depreciation}$$

5. Assume a structure is seven years old and has an effective age of five years. The appraiser estimates the total economic life at 50 years. If the reproduction cost new is $287,500, what is the accrued depreciation using the age-life method?

Cost Approach: Depreciation as a Percent

We can apply our T-device to assist with solving cost approach calculations. Depreciation may also be expressed as a percent. The total depreciation possible is 100 percent. If a structure were 100 percent depreciated, it would have no economic value.

To find the depreciation rate per year using the straight-line method, divide 100 percent (the total depreciation expressed as a percent) by the total years of useful life of the building:

part = total depreciation expressed as 100%

rate = annual percent of depreciation

total = total years of useful life

$$\frac{\text{Total depreciation (100\%)}}{\text{Total years of useful life} \quad \times \quad \text{Annual percent of depreciation}}$$

Hint: It may seem odd to label total depreciation of 100 percent as the part. Remember that depreciation is a "part" of the total useful life of a structure.

Example: A building has an estimated total useful life of 40 years. What is the annual rate of depreciation?

$$\text{part} = 100\%$$
$$\text{rate} = ?$$
$$\text{total} = 40 \text{ years}$$

$$\frac{100\%}{40 \text{ years} \times ?}$$

Therefore, it is estimated that the building loses 2.5 percent of its value per year.

Example: What would the estimated economic life of the above building have been if it were being depreciated at 2 percent per year?

Economic life = 100% (*part*) ÷ 2% per year (*rate*)

= 50 years (*total*)

$$\frac{100\%}{? \times 2\%}$$

The next two examples show how to find accrued depreciation as a percent and as an amount, once the annual depreciation rate is known.

Example: If the annual depreciation rate is 2.5 percent and the building has an effective age of eight years, what is the accrued depreciation expressed as a percent?

Accrued depreciation rate = 2.5% per year × 8 years = 20%

If the cost to reproduce the building new is $116,000, what is the accrued depreciation expressed as an amount?

Accrued depreciation rate = $116,000 × 20% = $23,200

The variables used in the above example to find accrued depreciation may be expressed as follows:

total = cost to reproduce new

rate = annual depreciation rate

time = effective age

part = accrued depreciation

$$\frac{\text{Accrued depreciation}}{\underset{\text{new}}{\text{Cost to reproduce}} \times \text{Depreciation rate} \times \text{Effective age}}$$

$$\frac{?}{\$116{,}000 \times 2.5\% \times 8 \text{ years}}$$

$$\text{Accrued depreciation} = \$116,000 \times 2.5\% \text{ per year} \times 8 \text{ years}$$
$$= \$23,200$$

Example: The estimated cost to reproduce a house is $75,000. Its current depreciated value has been estimated to be $61,500 with an effective age of six years. What is the annual rate of depreciation?

Begin by solving for the amount of accrued depreciation:

Total cost to reproduce	$75,000
Current depreciated value	− 61,500
Accrued depreciation	$13,500

$$\frac{\$13,500}{\$75,000 \times ? \times 6 \text{ years}}$$

The effective age is six years. Use this information to find the annual rate of depreciation:

$$\text{Annual rate of depreciation} = \$13,500 \div (\$75,000 \times 6 \text{ years})$$
$$= \$13,500 \div \$450,000$$
$$= .03 \text{ or } 3\%$$

Suppose you are asked to estimate the remaining current value of a building. Simply subtract the amount of accrued depreciation from the total cost to reproduce the building new.

From the previous example:

$$\text{Remaining current value} = \$116,000 - \$23,200$$
$$= \$92,800$$

Remaining current value (expressed as a percent) may be determined by first subtracting the accrued depreciation rate from the total cost to reproduce the building new, expressed as a percent (100%). Then multiply that remaining rate result times the dollar cost to reproduce the building new to find the remaining current value.

Again referring to the above example, in which the accrued depreciation rate was 20%:

$$\text{Remaining rate} = 100\% - 20\%$$
$$= 80\%$$

As shown in the memory device:

total = cost to reproduce

rate = remaining rate

part = remaining current value

$$\frac{\text{Remaining current value}}{\text{Cost to reproduce} \times \text{Remaining rate}}$$

Remaining current value $= \$116,000 \times 80\%$

$\qquad = \$92,800$

$$\frac{}{\$116,000} \div \frac{?}{} \div \frac{}{80\%}$$

The memory aid can also help with other common situations.

Example: The remaining current value of a building with an effective age of five years is $70,000, independent of land value. Originally, the economic life of the structure was estimated at 50 years. What is the cost to reproduce the building?

Remaining current value	$70,000
Economic life	50 years
Effective age of building	5 years
Total depreciation expressed as a percent	100%

By first expressing remaining current value (*part*) as a percent of the cost to reproduce (*rate*), the cost to reproduce (*total*) can then be found.

Find the annual depreciation rate:

Annual depreciation rate $= 100\% \div 50$ years $= 2\%$

Accrued depreciation rate $= 2\%$ annual depreciation rate $\times$ 5 years $= 10\%$

$$\frac{}{50 \text{ years}} \div \frac{100\%}{} \div \frac{}{?}$$

Remaining current value $= 100\% - 10\% = 90\%$

Cost to reproduce $= \$70,000 \div 90\% = \$77,777.78$
or $77,800 (rounded)

$$\frac{}{?} \div \frac{\$70,000}{} \div \frac{}{90\%}$$

Cost Approach: Practice Calculating Depreciation and Economic Life

Ok. Now it is time to see if you have mastered the arithmetic associated with the cost-depreciation approach. Calculate the economic life and the annual rate of depreciation as indicated below.

PRACTICE PROBLEMS

	Economic Life of Building	Annual Rate of Depreciation
6.	30 years	_____ %
7.	_____ years	4%
8.	_____ years	5%
9.	35 years	_____ %
10.	45 years	_____ %

Good job! Now you are ready to test your progress with several cost approach word problems.

11. A house has a chronological age of 12 years and an annual depreciation rate of 2 percent. The cost to reproduce the house new is $76,000. What is the current value of the house?

_____

12. An office building, when new, was estimated to have a useful life of 40 years. The depreciated value of the building, with an effective age of seven years, is estimated to be $148,500. Calculate the cost to reproduce the building.

_____

13. The remaining current value of a 10-year-old triplex has been appraised at $66,000. The cost to reproduce the triplex is $82,500. What is the annual rate of depreciation?

_____

14. A house cost $89,500 to build. When new, the building was estimated to have a 50-year useful life. Using straight-line depreciation, what is the accumulated depreciation after four years?

_____

15. You are appraising an industrial property for which the land value is estimated to be $80,000. The 15,000-square-foot building is six years old and had an economic life when new of 50 years. It would cost $32 per square foot to reproduce the structure today. The site location next to a paper mill has resulted in an external obsolescence depreciation of $19,000. What is the current estimated value of the property?

_____

16. A two-year-old apartment house would cost $134,000 to reproduce new. It had an estimated economic life of 50 years when new. The site on which the building stands is valued at $25,000. Estimate the total current value of the apartment house and land.

_____

17. You have been asked to estimate the market value of a building that has an effective age of six years. It would currently cost $125,000 to reproduce the structure new. The economic life is estimated to be 50 years and the land value is estimated to be $25,000. The building's original cost when new was $60,000. What is the estimated market value of the property using the age-life method to calculate depreciation?

_____

18. A house contains 2,300 square feet and would cost $85 per square foot to reproduce new. The land value is estimated to be $42,000. The effective age of the structure is six years and the estimated total economic life is 60 years. What is the estimated value of the property?

_____

19. The living area of a new two-story house measures 30' × 40'. The garage measures 15' × 30'. A utility room measures 8' × 10'. The house can be constructed for $75 per square foot, the garage for $45 per square foot, and the utility room for $40 per square foot. The site is estimated at $35,000. What is the value of the property?

SALES COMPARISON APPROACH

The *sales comparison approach* is based on the theory that a knowledgeable purchaser will pay no more for a property than the cost of acquiring an equally acceptable substitute property. The sales comparison approach is based on the premise that the value of a property can be estimated accurately by reviewing recent sales of properties known as **comparables.** The prices buyers are willing to pay for properties similar to the property of interest **(subject property)** gives an indication of what the property being appraised should bring in a competitive market.

The sales used for comparison purposes must meet two qualifications:

1. They must have occurred recently in the same market area where the subject property is located.

2. The comparable properties selected must be similar to the subject property.

Because no two properties are exactly alike, adjustments must be made for any differences between the subject property and each of the comparable sale properties. All adjustments necessary to achieve the maximum degree of similarity must be made to each comparable property, *not* to the subject property.

The intent is to adjust the comparable property to make it as similar to the subject property as possible. If a comparable property is *inferior* to the subject property on a given feature, an *upward* adjustment is made to that comparable property (add the value of the difference). If a comparable is *superior* on a given feature, a *downward* adjustment is made to the comparable property (subtract the value of the difference).

Example: The subject property is a three-bedroom, two-bath, two-car garage home with a pool.

A comparable property is a four-bedroom, two-bath, two-car garage home with no pool but it has a screened-in porch.

The appraiser estimates the value of each feature that requires an adjustment:

- Extra bedroom adds $15,000 value
- Pool adds $12,000 value
- Screened-in porch adds $2,000 value

If the comparable sold for $165,000, calculate the estimated market value of the subject property based on this information only.

Let's take one adjustment at a time. The subject property is a three-bedroom home. The comparable property is a four-bedroom home. The comparable is *superior* to the subject property with regard to the number of bedrooms. Therefore, the appraiser *subtracts* the value of the fourth bedroom from the sale price of the comparable.

The subject property has a pool valued at $12,000. The comparable property does not have a pool. The comparable property is *inferior* to the subject property with regard to the pool. Therefore, the appraiser *adds* the value of the pool to the sale price of the comparable.

The subject property does not have a screened-in porch. The comparable property has a screened-in porch valued at $2,000. The comparable property is *superior* to the subject property with regard to the porch. Therefore the appraiser *subtracts* the value of the screened-in porch from the sale price of the comparable.

Feature	Subject	Comparable	Value Adjustment
Bedrooms	3	4	($15,000)
Pool	Yes	No	+ $12,000
Porch	No	Yes	($2,000)

If we sum the adjustments we derive a net adjustment of *minus* $5,000. This amount is subtracted from the sale price of the comparable property.

Net adjustment = $5,000

$165,000 – $5,000 net adjustment = $160,000 estimated market value of subject property

PRACTICE PROBLEMS

Use the following information to calculate problems 20 through 23:

An appraiser is appraising a four-bedroom home with a swimming pool. Based on the appraiser's experience regarding the subject neighborhood, the appraiser estimates that a pool normally adds $15,000 in value to the property, and a bedroom adds about $20,000. The appraiser has located the following comparables:

Comp 1: five-bedrooms, no pool, sold for $155,000

Comp 2: four-bedrooms, no pool, sold for $132,000

Comp 3: three-bedrooms, pool, sold for $131,000

20. Calculate the adjusted sale price for Comp 1.

_____

21. Calculate the adjusted sale price for Comp 2.

_____

22. Calculate the adjusted sale price for Comp 3.

_____

23. The appraiser has determined that each of the comparables should be weighted equally. (Average the three adjusted sale prices.) What is the estimated value of the subject property based on the adjusted sale price of the three comparables?

_____

24. A single-family home is listed for sale. A comparable property sold for $95,000. The comparable has a superior location ($5,000); the comparable is newer by 10 years ($8,000) but has less square feet of livable area ($3,000). What is the adjusted sale price of the comparable?

Sales Comparison Approach: Estimating Site Value

The value of vacant lots is often estimated by reviewing the prices paid for similar neighboring lots. A common unit of comparison, such as cost per square foot or front foot, is used to equalize variations in value due to size and shape.

Example: What is the estimated market value of a subject lot that is 110 feet by 120 feet?

Recent comparable sales:

Sale 1: 100' × 120' lot located across the street from subject property, sold for $6,800

Sale 2: 110' × 120' lot in the same neighborhood as subject lot, sold for $7,000

Sale 3: 100' × 100' lot in a separate but similar quality neighborhood, sold for $6,000

Sale 4: 130' × 150' lot located in a similar neighborhood, sold for $9,800

	Price	Size		Price Per Sq. Ft.
Sale 1:	$6,800 ÷	12,000 sq. ft. =		$ .5667 per sq. ft.
Sale 2:	$7,000 ÷	13,200 sq. ft. =		.5303 per sq. ft.
Sale 3:	$6,000 ÷	10,000 sq. ft. =		.6000 per sq. ft.
Sale 4:	$9,800 ÷	19,500 sq. ft. =		.5026 per sq. ft.
				$2.1996

Average price per sq. ft. = $2.1996 ÷ 4 sales

= $ .5499 or $ .55 (rounded)

Note: An appraiser would typically consider which of the comparables are most like the subject property and place the greatest weight on those. For these examples, assume that all lots are equally desirable.

Square footage of subject lot (110' × 120')	13,200
Average price per square foot (comparables)	×$ .55
Estimated market value of subject lot	$7,260

PRACTICE PROBLEMS

25. What is the estimated market value of a subject lot measuring 90' × 120' if the following five comparables are of equal desirability?

Sale 1: Adjoins subject lot, measures 100' × 110', sold for $7,700

Sale 2: Across the street from subject lot, measures 90' × 110', sold for $6,850

Sale 3: On same street as subject lot in the next block, measures 110' × 110', sold for $8,590

Sale 4: A parcel two lots removed from the subject lot, measures 100' × 120', sold for $8,760

Sale 5: A lot in the next subdivision of similar quality as the subject lot, measures 100' × 120', sold for $8,650

Estimated market value of subject lot

INCOME CAPITALIZATION APPROACH

The *income capitalization approach* uses a **capitalization rate** and the projected net operating income to estimate property value.

The object of the income capitalization approach is to measure a flow of income projected into the future. The income capitalization approach develops an estimated market value based on the present worth of future income from the subject property. It is the primary approach for appraising income-producing property and for comparing possible investments.

The basic formula used by appraisers to solve income approach problems in real estate appraising is:

FORMULA

Income Approach

Net operating income ÷ Capitalization rate = Estimated property value

There is good news to report! We can use our trusty T-device to solve income capitalization rate calculations. Let's take another look at our formula and label each entry:

Part = Net income or expected return on investment

Rate = Capitalization rate

Total = Property value or total investment

$$\frac{\text{Net income}}{\text{Property value} \times \text{Capitalization rate}}$$

Therefore, using our T-device we know that:

Net operating income (*part*) ÷ Capitalization rate (*rate*) = Value (*total*)

Net operating income (NOI) is revenue from property or business after operating expenses have been deducted.

Relying once again on our T-device we can solve for NOI:

Capitalization rate (*rate*) × Value (*total*) = NOI (*part*)

For the purposes of this book, regard capitalization rate as a percent of return on the value of the investment. Referring to our T-device, we can see that if we know the property value and NOI, we can solve for the capitalization rate:

NOI (*part*) ÷ Property value (*total*) = Capitalization rate (*rate*)

Appraising is a complex process, and the focus here is limited to the basic arithmetic calculations of appraising. For now, the net operating income is provided for you. Later, we will discuss how to calculate the NOI.

Example: An apartment complex has an annual net income of $22,400. An appraiser has established a capitalization rate of 14 percent for this particular property. What would an investor be justified in paying for the property based on the capitalization rate and net operating income?

Total = _____

Rate = 14%

Part = $22,400

Property value = $22,400 ÷ 14%

= $160,000 (the amount an investor would be justified in paying)

$$\frac{\$22,400}{?\ \div\ \times\ 14\%}$$

26. The net operating income from a commercial building is $18,000. The estimated value of the property is $150,000. What capitalization rate did the appraiser use to arrive at this value?

_____

27. A small apartment building earns $14,000 net operating income per year. A knowledgeable investor requires at least a 12½ percent rate of return on her investment. What is the most the investor should pay for this property?

_____

28. A two-year-old apartment building produces an annual net income of $21,500. If you must have a 14 percent rate of return on your investment, what is the maximum you can pay for the apartment building and realize your 14 percent rate of return?

_____

You may be given income and expense data and be asked to find the net income of a property. Let's begin with a brief discussion of the various types of income you may be given in a word problem.

1. **Potential gross income** (PGI) is the total annual income a property would produce if it were fully rented and no collection losses were incurred.
2. **Effective gross income** (EGI) results when vacancy and collection losses are deducted from annual PGI.
3. **Net operating income** (NOI) is the income remaining after subtracting all relevant operating expenses from EGI.

Let's write out this information mathematically:

FORMULA

Net Operating Income

Potential gross income – Vacancy and collection losses = Effective gross income
Effective gross income – Operating expenses = Net operating income

Example: An apartment complex has 10 three-bedroom units renting for $525 per month and 40 two-bedroom units renting for $450 per month. Vacancy and collection losses in that area are expected to be approximately 5 percent. If the following expenses apply and a capitalization rate of 12.75 percent is used, what is the appraised value of the apartment complex?

Annual Expenses

Taxes	$37,500
Insurance	3,050
Maintenance	24,000
Management fee	25,400
Utilities	36,000
Trash and garbage	4,100
Reserve for replacements	33,000

The net operating income (*part*) must be found before the appraised value (*total*) can be found. Begin by solving for the **potential gross income** (PGI). The PGI assumes that every apartment is rented 100 percent of the time.

Income:

10 apts. @ $525/mo. × 12 months	$ 63,000
40 apts. @ $450/mo. × 12 months	+216,000
Potential gross income	$279,000

A deduction is then made for expected vacancies. Vacancy and collection losses are typically estimated as a percent of potential gross income (5 percent in this example). Vacancy and collection losses are subtracted from PGI to determine the **effective gross income** (EGI).

Potential gross income	$279,000
Estimated vacancy and collection losses (5% × $279,000)	– 13,950
Effective gross income	$265,050

Net operating income (NOI) is the income remaining after subtracting all relevant operating expenses from EGI. Operating expenses are grouped into three categories:

1. *Fixed expenses* are expenses that remain constant regardless of whether there are any vacancies. For example, fixed expenses include property taxes and hazard insurance.

2. *Variable expenses* are so named because the expense fluctuates with vacancies. Examples of variable expenses include utilities, maintenance, management, supplies, and so forth.

3. *Reserve for replacements* refers to a reserve allowance that provides for the periodic replacement of building components such as roof coverings and heating and air-conditioning equipment that wear out at a faster rate than structural components. In the following example, a reserve allowance of $33,000 is provided for replacing short-term building components.

Effective gross income		$265,050
Operating expenses		
1. Fixed expenses:		
Taxes	$37,500	
Insurance	3,050	
2. Variable expenses		
Maintenance	$24,000	
Management fee	25,400	
Utilities	36,000	
Trash and garbage	4,100	
3. Reserve for replacements	$33,000	
Total expenses:		−163,050
Net operating income:	$102,000	

Great. We now know the net operating income for our property. Recall that the question concerned the property value. We were given a capitalization rate of 12.75 percent. Let's plug the net operating income (*part*) and capitalization rate (*rate*) into our T-device:

Part = Net operating income = $102,000

Rate = Capitalization rate = 12.75%

Total = Appraised value = ?

$$\frac{\$102,000}{? \;\times\; 12.75\%}$$

$102,000 ÷ 12.75% = $800,000 appraised value

29. What is the value of a property based on the following information?

Potential gross income	$72,000
Vacancy and collection losses (6%)	
Operating expenses	
Management	$ 6,000
Maintenance	1,280
Utilities	7,600
Taxes	9,020
Insurance	1,100
Reserve for replacements	13,680
Trash removal	1,000
Capitalization rate 12.5%	

> **Hint:** When calculating income capitalization word problems, always convert monthly income and expenses into annual figures before applying the T-device.

30. Ten apartments rent for $450 per month each. Forty apartments rent for $395 per month each. Calculate the potential gross income.

31. Vacancy and collection losses are estimated to be 5 percent. Using the PGI calculated in problem 30, what is the effective gross income?

32. Fixed expenses totaled $28,340. Variable expenses totaled $53,450. Reserve for replacements totaled $18,900. Compute the net operating income, using the EGI calculated in problem 31.

33. Calculate the value of the rental property using a capitalization rate of 15 percent. Use the NOI calculated in problem 32.

GROSS RENT MULTIPLIER (GRM) AND GROSS INCOME MULTIPLIER (GIM)

A *gross rent multiplier* (GRM) is the ratio between a property's gross monthly rental income and its selling price. A *gross income multiplier* (GIM) is the ratio between a property's selling price and its gross annual income and which may also include income from sources other than rent. GRMs and GIMs convert gross income into market value.

To calculate either a gross rent multiplier or a gross income multiplier, information is collected from sales of similar properties. A relationship is then developed for each property by dividing each sale price by its monthly (GRM) or annual (GIM) gross rent.

FORMULA

Gross Rent Multiplier

Sale price ÷ Monthly gross rental income = Gross rent multiplier (GRM)

Gross Income Multiplier

Sale price ÷ Annual gross income = Gross income multiplier (GIM)

Example: The following is an illustration of the calculation of a gross rent multiplier using monthly rental income:

Sale	Sale Price	Monthly Rental	GRM
1	$89,100	$710	125.49
2	$84,420	$650	129.88
3	$90,785	$740	122.68
4	$87,750	$700	125.36
5	$92,480	$750	123.31

The average of the GRMs = 626.72 ÷ 5 = 125.34

An appraiser would apply an average GRM of 125 as a result of the above market analysis. The multiplier is then multiplied by the actual or expected monthly rental income produced from the property being appraised.

Example: Assume that you are appraising a rental property that produces monthly rent of $675. Apply the gross rent multiplier above to estimate the appraised value.

$675 Monthly rental income × 125 GRM = $84,375 Appraised value

---
PRACTICE PROBLEMS
---

34. You are appraising a rental property and have collected data from four comparable sales to establish a gross rent multiplier. Calculate the average gross rent multiplier.

Sale	Sale Price	Monthly Rental	GRM
1	$61,100	$470	_____
2	$62,225	$475	_____
3	$61,180	$460	_____
4	$60,970	$455	_____
		Average GRM =	_____

35. The rental property you are appraising has been renting for $470 per month. On the basis of the gross rent multiplier developed in practice problem 34, what is the estimated value of the rental property?

Estimated market value = _____

36. Calculate the market value of a fully occupied office building that is producing $210,000 annual gross income (round average multiplier to nearest tenth). Comparable property sales and income data reveal the following:

Sale	Sale Price	Annual Rental Income	GRM
1	$1,900,000	$216,000	_____
2	$1,575,000	$187,500	_____
3	$2,200,000	$256,700	_____
4	$1,750,000	$203,400	_____

Estimated market value = _____

FINANCIAL AND INVESTMENT ANALYSIS

We will now turn our attention to investment real estate. Before we go into financial and investment analysis of income-producing property, however, we will discuss some general real estate calculations associated with investment property such as calculating the IRS depreciation allowance.

Depreciation Allowance for Investment Real Estate

Depreciation is a means of deducting the costs of improvements to land over a specified period of time. The land itself is *not* depreciable. Depreciation (or cost recovery) allows taxpayers to recover the cost of depreciable property by paying less tax than they would otherwise have to pay. Under present tax law the depreciation deduction usually bears little relationship to actual changes in property value. Depreciation is used to stimulate economic expansion by making certain types of real property more attractive to investors. Depreciation is allowed only for business property and income-producing investment property.

> **Hint:** Do not confuse depreciation allowance with the cost approach to appraising. In the cost approach depreciation refers to the difference between the subject structure if new and the current condition of the structure for valuation purposes. IRS depreciation allowance is an on-paper deduction that is designed to encourage real estate investment. The annual deduction allowed for depreciation has no relationship to the actual physical condition of the investment property.

Depreciation allowance is calculated using the straight-line method. An equal amount of depreciation is taken annually. The IRS has currently established 27½ years as the depreciation period for residential rental property and 39 years for nonresidential income-producing property.

FORMULA

Annual Depreciation Allowance

Depreciable basis ÷ Number of years allowed by IRS =
Annual depreciation allowance

The *depreciable basis* is usually the purchase price minus the land value. Remember, we can only depreciate the structure.

Example: An investor purchased a residential rental property in January of this year for $350,000. The contract specified that the land was to be valued at 20 percent of the purchase price. What is the annual depreciation of this property?

Begin by determining the depreciable basis:

$$\$350,000 \times .80 = \$280,000$$

The investor uses the depreciable basis to calculate the annual depreciation allowance. The benefit of depreciation allowance is that it shields some of the income received from an investment from property taxation.

Because this is residential rental property, we must depreciate the structure using 27½ years:

$$\$280,000 \div 27\frac{1}{2} \text{ years} = \$10,182 \text{ annual depreciation}$$

What if instead the property was nonresidential income-producing property?

The only thing that changes is the number of years used in the straight-line method of calculating the depreciation allowance:

$$\$280,000 \div 39 \text{ years} = \$7,179 \text{ annual depreciation}$$

PRACTICE PROBLEMS

37.   Calculate the depreciation allowance for a residential rental property that was purchased in January for $250,000. The purchase price includes a land value of $40,000. (Round your answer to the nearest dollar.)

MULTISTEP INCOME TAX PROBLEMS

Sometimes word problems seem confusing because you aren't sure how to tackle the calculation. The next example is a multistep problem involving percentages.

Example: An investor is in a 33 percent tax bracket. The investor is considering four investments. Which investment would give the investor the best return?

12% after-tax

16% before-tax

10% after-tax

14% before-tax

What makes this problem difficult to understand is that we have been given rates of return rather than their dollar equivalent. We can easily eliminate two of the choices—a 10 percent after-tax return is obviously not as good as a 12 percent after-tax return and a 14 percent before-tax return (or pre-tax return) is less desirable compared with a 16 percent before-tax return. But we are still left with wondering which of the two remaining returns is better—a 12 percent after-tax return or a 16 percent before-tax return.

How are we going to figure out what a 16 percent before-tax return equates to after-tax based on a 33 percent tax bracket? Yikes! Let's see if we can make the numbers easier to understand. If we change percentage rates of return into dollar rates of return we will be able to apply the 33 percent. Simply change the percents into dollars like this:

> 12% after-tax: let's change this to $1,200 after-tax
> 16% before-tax: let's change this to $1,600 before-tax

We could have used $120 or $12,000 and $160 or $16,000. It doesn't really matter as long as we keep the relative value the same for both the 12 percent and 16 percent conversions.

To change the $1,600 before-tax return to after-tax return, multiply $1,600 by 33 percent:

$$\$1,600 \times .33 = \$528 \text{ taxes owed}$$

$$\$1,600 - \$528 = \$1,072 \text{ after-tax income}$$

Ok. Now what? Well let's work backwards.

Before we took 16 percent and made it $1,600, so we can express $1,072 as just under an 11 percent after-tax return.

Now we see that a 12 percent after-tax return is a better return compared with a 16 percent before-tax return.

PRACTICE PROBLEMS

38. An investor is in the 28 percent tax bracket. The investor is considering four investments. Which investment would give the investor the best return?

10% after-tax

12% pre-tax

8% after-tax

17% pre-tax

PERCENTAGE LEASES AND INDEXES

There are several types of leases that may be used with investment real estate. Two types of leases involve math calculations that are important to us.

A *percentage lease* is common in retail property. The lease provides for a proportional sharing of the monthly or annual gross sales made on the leased premises. There is typically a base or minimum monthly rent plus a percentage of the gross sales in excess of an amount specified in the lease.

Example: A lease calls for monthly minimum rent of $900 plus 3 percent of annual gross sales in excess of $270,000. What was the annual rent for the year if the annual gross sales were $350,600?

Begin by determining how much of the gross sales are subject to the 3 percent charge:

$350,600 total gross sales – $270,000 = $80,600 subject to 3% charge

Ok. So we know the amount of gross sales subject to the charge and we were given the 3 percent:

$80,600 × .03 = $2,418 additional annual rent

Lastly, we need to add the additional rent to the base rent. Note that the base rent was given as a monthly amount. We need to convert the base rent to an annual amount. Once the conversion to annual rent is completed, we simply add the annual base rent to the additional annual rent:

$900 per month base rent × 12 = $10,800 annual base rent
$10,800 + $2,418 = $13,218

How would you solve a problem that asked for the dollar amount of gross sales?

Example: A retail store is leased for $1,000 per month plus 3 percent of gross sales. The rent for the last month was $1,750. What were the gross sales for the month?

We know that the amount of sales subject to the 3 percent charge is the difference between last month's rent and the base rent.

$1,750 rent charged for month – $1,000 base rent =
$750 subject to 3% charge

So we know the rent and the rate. We can use our T-device to help us. The 3 percent is the *rate* and label the rent of $750 as the *part*. Solve for the gross sales (*total*).

$750 (part) ÷ .03 (rate) = $25,000 gross sales for the month

A variable lease features rent that changes at set times as specified in the lease agreement. A variable lease (or sometimes index lease) provides for adjustments of rent according to changes in a price index such as the consumer price index (CPI).

Example: A building rents for $8.00 per square foot with an index of 1.5. The index increases to 1.8. What is the renewal rental rate?

If the index was 1.5 and increases to 1.8, how much did prices increase?

1.8 – 1.5 = .3 difference
.3 ÷ 1.5 = 2, so prices increased by 20 percent

The renewal rate is the previous rent multiplied by the 20 percent increase:

$8.00 × 1.20 = $9.60 rent

Note: We could have also multiplied $8.00 by .20 = $1.60 and added this to the previous rent of $8.00. (See also page 24.)

PRACTICE PROBLEMS

39. A building rents for $10 per square foot with an index of 1.6. The index increases to 1.8. What is the renewal rental rate?

_____

40. A lease calls for monthly minimum rent of $750 plus 2 percent of annual gross sales in excess of $300,000. What was the annual rent for the year if the annual gross sales were $375,000?

_____

41. A retail store is leased for $1,500 per month plus 3 percent of gross sales. The rent for the last month was $1,950. How much were the gross sales for the month?

_____

TYPES OF INCOME USED IN INVESTMENT ANALYSIS

Financial and investment analysis provides a better grasp of the probable future economic health of selected income-producing properties. Our discussion here is limited to basic concepts required to conduct these analyses.

Investors are concerned with the income and expense projections of potential investments. This section of the chapter discusses the calculations associated with investment analysis. The first step in preparing an investment analysis is to estimate potential gross income based on the rents for comparable properties. Vacancy and collection losses are deducted, and other income is added, to determine the effective gross income. Operating expenses are estimated based on the owner's records and the analyst's forecast of future costs. The vacancy rate is based on competing properties in the same marketplace.

Do you recall our previous discussion of the various types of income mentioned above? Let's take a moment to review them now.

■ _Potential gross income_ (PGI) is the total income a property would produce if it were 100 percent rented and no collection losses were incurred (the first step in a financial analysis).

■ _Effective gross income_ (EGI) is the income produced after vacancy and collection losses are subtracted from potential gross income and any income from sources other than rent (for example, laundry and vending machines) is added (the second step in financial analysis).

■ _Net operating income_ (NOI) is the income remaining after deducting all operating expenses from effective gross income. NOI is the annual income _before_ mortgage and income tax payments. It is the basis for the income approach in appraising as well as for financial and investment analysis.

FORMULA

Effective Gross Income

Potential gross income – Vacancy and collection losses + Other income =
Effective gross income

Net Operating Income

Effective gross income – Operating expenses =
Net operating income

INVESTMENT ANALYSIS FOR BROKER CANDIDATES

Note: Most of the information in the rest of this chapter is tested exclusively on real estate broker exams. Check with your instructor regarding whether you may be tested on the material contained in this section.

Refer to the description of an investment property in the next paragraph. We will use this example throughout the rest of this chapter to conduct typical investment analysis calculations.

Example: Investor Bob purchased an apartment building in January for $295,000. He secured an 80 percent loan. The mortgage is for 30 years with an 8 percent interest rate and monthly payments of $1,731.68. The apartment complex consists of 10 apartments that rent for $500 a month and five apartments that rent for $450 a month. Collection losses are estimated at 10 percent, and operating expenses are estimated at 40 percent of the effective gross income.

Begin by calculating the potential gross income (PGI), effective gross income (EGI), and net operating income (NOI).

Calculate annual rental income assuming 100 percent occupancy.

$$10 \text{ units} \times \$500 \text{ rent} \times 12 \text{ months} = \$60,000$$
$$5 \text{ units} \times \$450 \text{ rent} \times 12 \text{ months} = \underline{\$27,000}$$
$$\text{Total PGI} = \$87,000$$

Deduct estimated vacancy and collection loss from PGI.

$$\$87,000 \times .10 = \underline{- \ 8,700}$$
$$\text{EGI} = \$78,300$$

Subtract expenses from EGI.

$$\$78,300 \times .40 = \underline{- 31,320}$$
$$\text{NOI} = \$46,980$$

An appraiser is concerned primarily with capitalizing net operating income into value. However, investors and lenders are typically more interested in the cash flow before and after taxes.

Before-tax cash flow or cash throw-off is the amount that results when annual debt service (mortgage payments) is subtracted from NOI. Net operating income does not take into consideration the cost of financing the real estate. Before-tax cash flow gives a better picture of how much money will be left after expenses and debt service are paid.

FORMULA

Before-Tax Cash Flow

Net operating income − Annual debt service expense =
Before-tax cash flow

Subtract annual mortgage expense from NOI.

$$NOI = \$46,980$$
$$\$1,731.68 \times 12 \text{ months} = -\underline{20,780}$$
$$\text{Before-tax cash flow} = \overline{\$26,200}$$

So we have determined that investor Bob has an annual cash flow of $26,200 remaining after paying the operating expenses and mortgage expense. Now we turn our attention to several financial ratios used by lenders and investors to evaluate the quality of an investment.

PREDICTING FUTURE RETURN RATES AND ECONOMIC RATIOS

Using the estimates of an investment's income, expense, debt service, and before-tax cash flow, several important rates and ratios can be calculated. The primary purpose of investment ratios is to allow comparisons between alternative investment properties before purchase and to predict future rates of return to an investor. Rate of return calculations relate NOI to capital investment in land and buildings.

We begin by calculating the equity dividend rate. *Equity dividend rate* is also referred to as the cash-on-cash return. It is the first-year relationship between the amount of cash remaining after annual debt-service costs (mortgage payments) and invested capital or down payment. Therefore it is a rate of return on invested capital (or equity).

FORMULA

Equity Dividend Rate

First year before-tax cash flow ÷ Down payment =
Equity dividend rate

Divide Bob's before-tax cash flow in the previous example by down payment (equity).

$$\text{Before tax cash flow} = \$26,200$$

$$\$295,000 \times .20 \text{ down} = \$59,000$$

$$\text{Equity dividend rate} = \$26,200 \div \$59,000 = .444 \text{ or } 44.4\%$$

This is a very high equity dividend rate indeed! Most investors are looking for a more realistic equity dividend rate of 12 percent to 20 percent. An equity dividend rate of 44 percent sure would be a great argument for investing in real estate!

The *debt service coverage ratio* (DSCR) is the ratio of a property's net operating income to its annual debt service. Lenders usually specify a minimum debt service coverage ratio (such as 1.20) that they require the property to meet during the first year of a loan term. The higher the ratio, the less risk to the lender.

Debt Service Coverage Ratio

Net operating income ÷ Annual debt service = Debt service coverage ratio

Divide NOI by annual mortgage payments.

Debt service coverage ratio = $46,980 NOI ÷ $20,780 = 2.26

A lender would feel secure with this debt service coverage ratio. In Investor Bob's case, the ratio is high for two reasons: (1) the net operating income is substantial, and (2) the debt service is low due to the owner's equity and low mortgage interest rate.

The *operating expense ratio* is the relationship between operating expenses and effective gross income. The lower the ratio, the less risk faced by the investor.

Operating Expense Ratio

Operating expenses ÷ Effective gross income = Operating expense ratio

Divide operating expenses by effective gross income.

Operating expense ratio = $31,320 ÷ $78,300 = .40

This is a high operating expense ratio. Investor Bob must feel confident that the expense estimates are not understated. Otherwise, Investor Bob may be unable to pay all of the expense associated with the property from income earned.

The *cash break-even ratio* is the relationship between total cash outlay costs and PGI. At 100 percent, expenses would equal potential income. In other words, the property would have to be 100 percent occupied for the investor to meet all of the expenses associated with the property including debt service. Reserve for replacements are not included in the operating expenses because it is non-expended money set aside for replacing items that wear out. The expenses used in the ratio are out-of-pocket expenses.

Cash Break-Even Ratio

Operating expenses – Reserve for replacements + Annual mortgage payment ÷ Potential gross income = Cash break-even ratio

(Note: In this example, we do not have a figure for reserves.)

$31,320 + $20,780 = $52,100

Divide this figure by PGI.

$52,100 ÷ $87,000 = .5988 or 59.9%

Investor Bob could pay the operating expenses and mortgage expense from the income generated from the property as long as the property is at least 60% occupied.

Use the following information to answer problems 42 through 52:

An investor purchased an apartment building in January for $250,000. The contract specified that $200,000 of the purchase price was allocated to the building and $50,000 of the purchase price was for the land. The investor made a down payment of $50,000 and financed the remainder of the purchase with a loan. The mortgage is for 30 years at 8 percent interest with a monthly payment of $1,467.53. The apartment building consists of 11 apartments that rent for $400 per month. Vacancy and collection losses are estimated at 6 percent. Operating expenses are 30 percent of the effective gross income and include reserves of $5,000.

Calculate the following:

42. PGI

_____

43. EGI

_____

44. Operating expenses

_____

45. NOI

_____

46. Annual debt service

_____

47. Debt service coverage ratio

_____

48. Before-tax cash flow

_____

49. Operating expense ratio

_____

50. Equity dividend rate

_____

51. Annual IRS depreciation allowance

_____

52. Cash break-even ratio

_____

ANSWER KEY

1. $60' \times 35' = 2{,}100$ square feet $\times \$80 = \$168{,}000$;
   $22' \times 25' = 550$ square feet $\times \$42.00 = \$23{,}100$;
   $\$168{,}000 + \$23{,}100 = \$191{,}100$ reproduction cost new

2. $\$191{,}100 \div 50$ years economic life =
   $\$3{,}822$ annual depreciation

3. $\$3{,}822$ annual depreciation $\times 6$ years =
   $\$22{,}932$ accrued depreciation

4. $\$191{,}100$ reproduction cost new $- \$22{,}932$
   accrued depreciation $+ \$25{,}000$ site value =
   $\$193{,}168$ (or $\$193{,}200$ rounded to nearest $\$100$)
   estimated property value

5. $\$287{,}500 \times$ (5 effective age $\div 50$ total economic
   life) $= \$287{,}500 \times .10 = \$28{,}750$ accrued
   depreciation

6. 100% (*part*) $\div 30$ years (*total*) =
   $.0333$ or 3.33% per year (*rate*)

7. 100% (*part*) $\div 4\%$ per year (*rate*) =
   25 years (*total*)

8. 100% (*part*) $\div 5\%$ per year (*rate*) =
   20 years (*total*)

9. 100% (*part*) $\div 35$ years (*total*) =
   $.02857$ or 2.86% per year (*rate*)

10. 100% (*part*) $\div 45$ years (*total*) =
    $.0222$ or 2.22% per year (*rate*)

11. 12 years chronological age $\times 2\%$ =
    24% accrued depreciation rate;
    $\$76{,}000 \times .24 = \$18{,}240$ accrued depreciation;
    $\$76{,}000 - \$18{,}240 = \$57{,}760$ current value

12. 100% (*part*) $\div 40$ years (*total*) =
    2.5% per year (*rate*);
    7 years effective age $\times 2.5\%$ =
    17.5% total depreciation as a percent;
    $100\% - 17.5\% = 82.5\%$ not depreciated;
    $\$148{,}500 \div .825 = \$180{,}000$ reproduction cost

13. $\$82{,}500$ cost to reproduce $- \$66{,}000$ value =
    $\$16{,}500$ accrued depreciation;
    $\$16{,}500 \div 10$ years $= \$1{,}650$ annual depreciation;
    $\$1{,}650$ (*part*) $\div \$82{,}500$ (*total*) =
    $.02$, or 2%, annual rate of depreciation (*rate*)

14. 100% (*part*) $\div 50$ years (*total*) =
    2% per year (*rate*)
    4 years $\times 2\% = 8\%$
    $\$89{,}500 \times .08 = \$7{,}160$ accumulated depreciation

15. 100% (*part*) $\div 50$ years (*total*) =
    2% per year (*rate*);
    6 years $\times 2\% = 12\%$;
    $15{,}000$ sq. ft. $\times \$32$ per sq. ft. =
    $\$480{,}000$ reproduction cost new;
    $\$480{,}000 \times .12 = \$57{,}600$;
    $\$57{,}600 + \$19{,}000$ external obsolescence =
    $\$76{,}600$ total depreciation;
    $\$480{,}000 - \$76{,}600 =$
    $\$403{,}400$ depreciated value of building;
    $\$403{,}400 + \$80{,}000$ land value =
    $\$483{,}400$ estimated property value

16. 100% (*part*) $\div 50$ years (*total*) =
    2% per year (*rate*);
    2 years $\times 2\% = 4\%$;
    $\$134{,}000$ reproduction cost new $\times .04 =$
    $\$5{,}360$ depreciation;
    $\$134{,}000 - \$5{,}360 =$
    $\$128{,}640$ depreciated value of building;
    $\$128{,}640 + \$25{,}000$ land =
    $\$153{,}640$ estimated property value

17. $\$125{,}000$ ($6 \div 50$) = accrued depreciation;
    $\$125{,}000 \times .12 = \$15{,}000$ accrued depreciation;
    $\$125{,}000$ reproduction cost new $- \$15{,}000$
    depreciation $+ \$25{,}000$ land $= \$135{,}000$

18. $2{,}300$ square feet $\times \$85 =$
    $\$195{,}500$ reproduction cost new;
    $\$195{,}500 \times (6 \div 60) = \$195{,}500 \times .10 =$
    $\$19{,}550$ depreciation;
    $\$195{,}500 - \$19{,}550 + \$42{,}000$ land =
    $\$217{,}950$ property value or $\$218{,}000$ (rounded to
    nearest $\$100$)

19. $30' \times 40' = 1{,}200$ square feet $\times 2$ stories =
    $2{,}400$ square feet living area;
    $15' \times 30' = 450$ square feet garage area;
    $8' \times 10' = 80$ square feet utility room area;
    $2{,}400 \times \$75 =$
    $\$180{,}000$ reproduction cost living area;
    $450 \times \$45 =$
    $\$20{,}250$ reproduction cost garage area;
    $80 \times \$40 =$
    $\$3{,}200$ reproduction cost utility room area;
    $\$180{,}000 + \$20{,}250 + \$3{,}200 =$
    $\$203{,}450$ reproduction cost new;
    $\$203{,}450 + \$35{,}000$ land =
    $\$238{,}450$ property value

20. Comp 1 is superior with regard to bedrooms (–$20,000) and is inferior with regard to a pool (+$15,000); ($20,000) + $15,000 = ($5,000); $155,000 sale price – $5,000 = $150,000 adjusted sale price

21. Comp 2 is inferior to the subject with regard to a pool (+$15,000); $132,000 sale price + $15,000 = $147,000

22. Comp 3 is inferior with regard to bedrooms (+$20,000); $131,000 + $20,000 = $151,000

23. $150,000 + $147,000 + $151,000 = $448,000 ÷ 3 comps = $149,333.33 or $149,300 (rounded to nearest $100)

24. $95,000 – $5,000 – $8,000 + $3,000 = $85,000 adjusted sale price

25. Sale 1: 100' × 110' = 11,000 sq. ft.; $7,700 ÷ 11,000 sq. ft = $.70 per sq. ft; Sale 2: 90' × 110' = 9,900 sq. ft.; $6,850 ÷ 9,900 sq. ft. = $.6919 per sq. ft.; Sale 3: 110' × 110' = 12,100 sq. ft.; $8,590 ÷ 12,100 sq. ft. = $.7099 per sq. ft.; Sale 4: 100' × 120' = 12,000 sq. ft.; $8,760 ÷ 12,000 sq. ft. = $.73 per sq. ft.; Sale 5: 100' × 120' = 12,000 sq. ft.; $8,650 ÷ 12,000 sq. ft. = $.7208 per sq. ft.; $.7000 + $.6919 + $.7099 + $.7300 + $.7208 = $3.5526; $3.5526 ÷ 5 sales = $.7105 or $.71 (rounded); Subject: 90' × 120' = 10,800 sq. ft. × $.71/sq. ft. = $7,668 value

26. $18,000 NOI (*part*) ÷ $150,000 value (*total*) = .12 or 12% cap rate (*rate*)

27. $14,000 NOI (*part*) ÷ .125 (*rate*) = $112,000 (*total*)

28. $21,500 NOI (*part*) ÷ .14 (*rate*) = $153,571.43 value (*total*) or $153,600 (rounded to nearest $100)

29. $72,000 PGI (*total*) × .06 (*rate*) = $4,320 (vacancy and collection losses) (*part*); $72,000 PGI – $4,320 V&C = $67,680 EGI; $67,680 – $39,680 operating expenses = $28,000 NOI; $28,000 NOI (*part*) ÷ .125 (*rate*) = $224,000 value (*total*)

30. $450 × 12 months × 10 units = $54,000; $395 × 12 months × 40 units = $189,600; $54,000 + $189,600 = $243,600 PGI

31. $243,600 PGI × .05 V&C = $12,180 V&C; $243,600 – $12,180 = $231,420 EGI

32. $28,340 + $53,450 + $18,900 = $100,690 total operating expenses; $231,420 EGI – $100,690 operating expenses = $130,730 NOI

33. $130,730 NOI ÷ .15 = $871,533.33 value, or $871,500 (rounded to nearest $100)

34. Sale 1: $61,100 ÷ $470 = 130 GRM; Sale 2: $62,225 ÷ $475 = 131 GRM; Sale 3: $61,180 ÷ $460 = 133 GRM; Sale 4: $60,970 ÷ $455 = 134 GRM; 130 + 131 + 133 + 134 = 528; 528 ÷ 4 sales = 132 average GRM

35. 132 GRM × $470 rent = $62,040 value

36. Sale 1: $1,900,000 ÷ $216,000 = 8.796 = 8.8 (rounded); Sale 2: $1,575,000 ÷ $187,500 = 8.4; Sale 3: $2,200,000 ÷ $256,700 = 8.57 = 8.6 (rounded); Sale 4: $1,750,000 ÷ $203,400 = 8.6; 8.8 + 8.4 + 8.6 + 8.6 = 34.4; 34.4 ÷ 4 sales = 8.6 average GIM; $210,000 annual gross income × 8.6 = $1,806,000 value

37. $250,000 – $40,000 land = $210,000 depreciable basis; $210,000 ÷ 27.5 years = $7,636

38. Eliminate 8% after-tax and 12% pre-tax; Let 17% pre-tax be $1,700; Let 10% after-tax be $1,000; $1,700 × .28 = $476 taxes due; $1,700 – $476 = $1,224; $1,224 compares to just over 12%; So 17% pre-tax is a better return compared with 10% after-tax

39. 1.8 – 1.6 = .2 difference; .2 ÷ 1.6 = .125; $10 × 1.125 = $11.25 renewal rental rate

40. $375,000 – $300,000 = $75,000 sales subject to 2% charge; $75,000 × .02 = $1,500 additional rent charged; $750 × 12 = $9,000 base annual rent; $9,000 + $1,500 = $10,500 total annual rent charged

41. $1,950 − $1,500 =
$450 rent subject to 3 percent charge;
$450 (*part*) ÷ .03 (*rate*) =
$15,000 gross sales (*total*)

42. $400 × 11 units × 12 = $52,800 PGI

43. $52,800 PGI × .06 = $3,168 V&C;
$52,800 − $3,168 = $49,632 EGI

44. $49,632 EGI × .30 = $14,890 operating expenses

45. $49,632 EGI − $14,890 = $34,742 NOI

46. $1,467.53 mortgage payment × 12 mos. =
$17,610 debt service

47. $34,742 NOI ÷ $17,610 annual debt service =
1.97

48. $34,742 NOI − $17,610 annual debt service =
$17,132 before-tax cash flow

49. $14,890 operating expenses ÷ $49,632 EGI = .30

50. $17,132 before-tax cash flow ÷ $50,000 down
payment = .343 or 34.3%

51. $250,000 purchase price − $50,000 land =
$200,000 depreciable basis;
$200,000 ÷ 27.5 years = $7,273

52. $14,890 operating expenses − $5,000 reserves +
$17,610 annual debt service = $27,500;
$27,500 ÷ $52,800 PGI = .521 or 52.1

Chapter Eight

COMPUTATIONS AND CLOSING STATEMENTS

Arrears paid at the end of the period for which payment is due (the opposite of *in advance*)

Credit an amount in favor of either the buyer or the seller

Debit a charge against the buyer or the seller

Prorate to divide or assess proportionate shares of expenses between the buyer and seller according to their individual period of ownership

Title Closing final settlement between the buyer and seller when title passes from the seller to the buyer

Chapter | **Overview**

At the **title closing,** the seller delivers title to the buyer in exchange for the purchase price. The sale contract specifies the date of closing and designates responsibility for payment of closing cost items. This chapter explains and illustrates how to determine the debits and credits that must be shown on the closing statement.

PRORATING

To **prorate** means to divide various charges and credits between buyer and seller. Every sale contract should specify a date and time for prorating items. It is customary when transferring title to have all prorated items determined as of midnight prior to the date of closing. This means that:

1. The buyer is *charged* for property taxes on the day of closing
2. The buyer is *charged* for interest on an assumed mortgage on the day of closing
3. The buyer is *credited* for any rental income earned on the day of closing

In some states it is customary for the seller to be responsible for charges incurred on the day of closing. In reality whether the buyer or seller pays any of the closing costs is *negotiable,* including the party responsible for the day of closing.

> **Hint:** Read each test question carefully. If the party charged for the day of closing is *not* the person customarily charged in your state, the license exam question will indicate who is to be charged (or credited) for the day of closing.

You may be required to prorate rent, property taxes, or mortgage interest. Rent is typically paid on a monthly basis at the beginning of the month (prepaid). Property taxes are paid in **arrears** (at the end of the period for which payment is due). Monthly mortgage payments are typically paid in arrears. Only the interest portion is prorated.

Prorated items are entered on the closing statement as *double entries.* Each prorated item is entered on the closing statement as a **debit** (charge) to one party and as a **credit** (income) to the other party.

It may be helpful to regard the terms *debit* and *credit* as simply headings for columns of data. Under the heading *debit* are included amounts that are owed at closing. Under the heading *credit* are included amounts that are to be received at closing. These terms apply to both buyer and seller when prorating. For example, if the buyer owes the seller $50, the buyer is debited $50 and the seller is credited $50. If the seller owes the buyer $50, the seller is debited $50 and the buyer is credited $50.

Hint: The dollar amount of the debit and credit is always identical (the same value) for a particular proration. Any answer choices to a proration test question that state a different dollar amount for the debit and credit can be immediately eliminated as an answer choice.

To prorate costs, two methods may be used: the *30-day-month method* and the *365-day method*. The two methods are explained below.

Prorating: 30-Day-Month Method

In this method, all months are considered to have 30 days (even February). Let's begin with an example that concerns a single month.

To use this method, first divide the monthly cost of the item by 30 to find the exact daily rate. Next multiply the number of days involved by the daily rate.

FORMULA

30-Day-Month Method

Total cost or income ÷ 30 Days = Daily cost or income

Daily cost or income × Total days transferred = Prorated cost or income

Example: If the monthly rental income is $180, what is the daily rent?

Divide the rent income by 30 days to determine the rent per day:

$180 ÷ 30 days = $6 per day

Example: Assume a closing date of June 15. How much is the seller to pay the buyer for the unused portion of the advance rent? (The day of closing belongs to the buyer.)

Multiply the rent per day by the number of days of unused rent due the buyer:

30 days in the month – 14 days used portion = 16 days unused portion

$6 per day × 16 days = $96

PRACTICE PROBLEMS

1. Rental income is $930 per month. What is the rent per day?

_____

2. Closing date is December 10. The day of closing belongs to the buyer. How many days of unused rental income is owed to the buyer?

_____

3. Using the information in problems 1 and 2, calculate the dollar amount of the proration based on the number of days' rent owed to the buyer.

_____

The 30-day method is also called the *360-day-statutory-year* method. When the proration is over a one-year period each month is considered to have 30 days. To use this method, first divide the annual cost of the item by 360 to find the exact daily rate. Next multiply the number of days involved by the daily rate.

FORMULA

360-Day-Statutory-Year Method

Total cost or income ÷ 360 Days = Daily cost or income

Daily cost or income × Total days transferred = Prorated cost or income

Example: If the total annual cost of an item is $3,600, what is the daily cost of the item, assuming a 360-day year?

Divide the annual cost by 360 days to determine the cost per day:

$3,600 ÷ 360 days = $10 per day

Example: Assume a closing date of March 1. Using the number of days from January 1 through midnight March 1, what is the prorated amount?

Multiply the cost per day calculated in the previous example by the number of days in the period January 1 through midnight March 1, assuming a 360-day year.

January (30) + February (30) + one day in March = 61 days

$10 per day × 61 days = $610

PRACTICE PROBLEMS

4. Closing date is April 20. How many days are in the period beginning January 1 and ending midnight of April 19?

_____

5. If the annual cost of an item is $3,600, what is the dollar amount of the proration for the period January 1 and ending midnight of April 19?

_____

Prorating: 365-Day Year Method

To use this method, first divide the annual cost of the item by 365 (the actual number of days in a year) to find the exact daily rate. (Note: If the exam question indicated that it was a leap year, February would have 29 days and the total number of days for the year would be 366.) Next multiply the number of days involved by the daily rate.

FORMULA

365-Day-Year Method

Total cost or income ÷ 365 Days = Daily cost or income

Daily cost or income × Total days transferred = Prorated cost or income

Example: If the total cost of an item is $1,500, what is the daily cost?

$1,500 ÷ 365 days = $4.109589 per day

Example: Assume a closing date of February 14. Using the number of days from January 1 through midnight February 14, what is the prorated amount?

January (31) + February (14) = 45 total days

45 days × $4.109589 per day = $184.93151 or $184.93 rounded

An alternative procedure for prorating with the 365-day method is:

365-Day-Year Alternative Method

Exact number of days ÷ 365 Days × Total cost = Prorated cost

Example: Use the previous example.

$$(45 \text{ days} \div 365 \text{ days}) \times \$1,500 = .1232877 \times \$1,500 = \$184.93151$$
$$= \$184.93 \text{ (rounded)}$$

> **Hint:** The 365-day method is the most accurate method. Use this method unless the exam question indicates that you are to use the 30-day (360) method.

Example: Consider a transaction scheduled to close on July 15 of a 365-day year. Property taxes for the year are estimated to be $986 and are to be prorated between seller and buyer. Day of closing belongs to the buyer.

Property taxes are normally paid at the end of the year (in arrears). Therefore, the taxes have not yet been paid. The seller owes the buyer for the seller's period of ownership.

Step 1   Calculate the average cost per day.

$986 property tax ÷ 365 days = $2.7013698 cost per day

Step 2   Calculate the number of the seller's days of ownership.

January (31) + February (28) + March (31) + April (30) + May (31) + June (30) + July (14) = 195 days

Step 3   Calculate the prorated cost.

$2.7013698 × 195 days = $526.76711 or $526.77

The seller owes the buyer $526.77. On the closing statement, the seller will be *debited* $526.77 and the buyer will be *credited* $526.77.

> **Hint:** When prorating, always consider whether the expense involved is *paid in advance* (as with rental income) or *paid in arrears* (as with property taxes). If the expense is paid in advance, calculate the days owed the buyer (buyer's days of ownership). If the expense is paid in arrears, calculate the days the seller must reimburse the buyer (seller's days of ownership).

The proration calculation should reflect the actual number of days a property was owned by the seller. It may be helpful to use a memory technique for recalling the number of days in each month. Some people rely on this simple Mother Goose rhyme:

> Thirty days hath September,
>
> April, June, and November;
>
> February has twenty-eight alone,
>
> All the rest have thirty-one;
>
> Excepting leap year, that's the time,
>
> When February's days are twenty-nine.

Others prefer to use the "knuckle method" for recalling the number of days in a month. Make each hand into a fist as shown below. Begin with the knuckle of the little finger on your left hand, which will be named January, and move from left to right assigning the names of the month to each knuckle and each valley as follows:

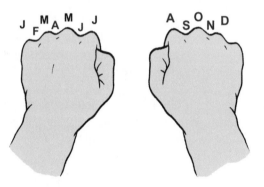

Note that all knuckles represent 31-day months. The valleys between the knuckles represent 30-day months, except for February, which everyone remembers has only 28 days (29 in a leap year).

Example: If a closing is scheduled for July 20 of a 365-day year, taxes should be allocated as follows: (Assume the property taxes are paid in arrears.)

Days:	31	28	31	30	31	30	31	31	30	31	30	31
Month:	J	F	M	A	M	J	J	A	S	O	N	D
Owned:			Seller: 200 days							Buyer: 165 days		

July
20

PRACTICE PROBLEMS

How many days are represented by the following periods of time in 365-day years?

6. January 1 to midnight, March 6:_____ days

7. December 21 to midnight, July 29:_____ days

8. March 4 to midnight, August 17: _____ days

PRORATING PROPERTY TAXES

In some states, for example Florida, property taxes are paid in arrears (at the end of the tax year). The seller has had possession and use of the property for some portion of the year, unless the transfer of title was effective on January 1. To apportion the property taxes fairly, they are prorated on the basis of a 365- (or 366-) day year.

To calculate a property tax proration, use the following procedure:

1. The total annual tax assessment is divided by the number of days in the year to determine the tax cost per day.

2. The property tax chargeable to the seller, on departure from the property, is calculated by multiplying the tax cost per day by the number of calendar days before title is conveyed.

3. The resulting amount is entered on the seller's closing statement as a *debit*. It is also shown on the buyer's closing statement, but as a *credit*. The buyer's share of property taxes is not reflected on either closing statement because he or she will not be required to settle the tax bill at closing.

FORMULA

Property Tax Proration

Total tax assessment ÷ 365 (or 366) days = Tax cost per day

Tax cost per day × Days of seller ownership = Prorated tax cost to the seller

Example: The closing date for a transaction was May 12. The tax year runs from January 1 through December 31. The estimated taxes are $1,168. The day of closing is charged to the buyer. How should the taxes be prorated?

Step 1   Calculate the tax cost per day.

$1,168 ÷ 365 days = $3.20 daily tax cost

Step 2   Determine the number of days the seller owned the property in the tax year.

January (31) + February (28) + March (31) + April (30) + May (11) = 131 days of seller ownership

The seller pays the property taxes owed for the seller's days of ownership at closing.

Step 3   Tax cost per day times days of seller's ownership equals the prorated tax cost of the seller.

$3.20 × 131 days = $419.20 (owed to buyer from seller)

Debit the seller $419.20
Credit the buyer $419.20

PRACTICE PROBLEMS

9. Closing will be on October 16. Estimated taxes are $876, and your broker has asked you to tell the buyer and the seller what each will owe or receive credit for at closing. How do you allocate the property taxes?

Debit the _____ $ _____

Credit the _____ $ _____

Note: It is possible that you will be required to calculate the property tax bill *before* you can calculate the proration.

Example: The estimated tax rate for the city is 5 mills, the county tax rate is 8.5 mills, and the school board rate is 2.5 mills. The taxable value of the property is estimated to be $50,000. The property closes on April 30 with the day of closing belonging to the seller. Calculate the tax proration.

Step 1   Calculate the total mills.

5 + 8.5 + 2.5 = 16 mills (or in decimal form .016)

Step 2   Multiply the taxable value by the millage rate to determine the annual property taxes.

$50,000 × .016 = $800

Step 3   Calculate the daily tax cost.

$800 ÷ 365 = $2.1918

Step 4   Calculate the number of seller days owed.

January (31) + February (28) + March (31) + April (30) = 120 days

Step 5   Calculate the proration amount.

$2.1918 × 120 days = $263.02 (rounded)

Debit the seller $263.02
Credit the buyer $263.02

Hint: Incorrect answers typically are based on (1) the day of closing is not assigned to the correct party; (2) the persons to receive the debit and the credit are reversed, and (3) the wrong side of the timeline is calculated. Therefore, *before* doing the math, consider whether the item is prepaid or paid in arrears, and who is debited and who is credited.

Property taxes are normally prorated using the 365-day method and the buyer is charged for property taxes on the day of closing. However, read the exam question carefully and follow the instructions. For example, in the previous example the seller was charged for property taxes on the day of closing.

PRACTICE PROBLEMS

10. Closing is on September 16. Estimated taxes are $1,876. The seller owns the day of closing. Use the 360-day method. How are the property taxes allocated on the closing statement?

Debit the _____ $ _____

Credit the _____ $ _____

> **Hint:** State exam calculations generally are not rounded off until the end of the calculation. Round off prorations to the penny.

PRORATING RENT

Normally, any rental income collected in advance belongs to the new owner as of the date of closing. Therefore, the unused portion of advance rent belongs to the buyer. The total rent amount is divided by the number of days involved in the rental period and allocated on a daily basis.

FORMULA

Rent Proration

Total rent ÷ Number of days in rental period = Average rental income per day

Average rent per day × Days due the buyer = Prorated buyer's share

Example: Assume that a property rents for $475 per month. The closing date is on the 21st day of a 31-day month. Day of closing belongs to the buyer. The proration would be as follows:

$$\$475 \div 31 \text{ days} = \$15.32258 \text{ per day}$$

$$31 \text{ days} - 20 \text{ used seller days} = 11 \text{ unused days owed buyer}$$

$$\$15.32258 \times 11 \text{ days} = \$168.54838, \text{ or}$$

$$\$168.55 \text{ due buyer from seller}$$

This exact amount involved must be accounted for on the closing statement. Because the seller has already collected the rent in advance, the seller owes the buyer (*debit* the seller $168.55; *credit* the buyer $168.55).

PRACTICE PROBLEMS

11. Closing date is April 20 for the sale of a five-unit apartment building. Rental income per unit is $360 per month. Day of closing belongs to the seller. Calculate the proration amount.

Broker exam candidates may be required to calculate a rent proration that also includes a security deposit. The security deposits do not belong to the seller. The entire amount of the security deposits is transferred to the new owner on behalf of the tenants.

Example: The sale of an apartment complex is scheduled to close on March 14. The complex contains 10 units, which rent for $550 per unit. The seller is also holding security deposits in the amount of $400 per unit. Day of closing belongs to the seller.

$$\$550 \text{ per unit} \times 10 \text{ units} = \$5,500 \text{ total monthly rent}$$

$$\$5,500 \text{ rent} \div 31 \text{ days in March} = \$177.41935 \text{ daily rent}$$

$$31 \text{ days in March} - 14 \text{ seller days} = 17 \text{ unused days owed buyer}$$

$$\$177.41935 \times 17 \text{ days } = \$3{,}016.13 \text{ (rounded)}$$

$$\$400 \times 10 \text{ units } = \$4{,}000 \text{ security deposits}$$

$$\$4{,}000 \text{ security deposits} + \$3{,}016.13 \text{ rent } = \$7{,}016.13 \text{ prorated amount}$$
$$\text{(debit seller; credit buyer)}$$

Sometimes rent begins on a date other than the first of the month. For example, how many days rent is in the period February 12 through March 11? To calculate the number of days, begin with the month of February:

$$28 \text{ days in February} - 11 \text{ days not counted } = 17 \text{ days counted}$$

$$11 \text{ days in March} + 17 \text{ days in February } = 28 \text{ days in period}$$

Example: Assume that a property rents for $890 per month. The rental period runs from July 15 through August 14. The closing date is on July 28. The day of closing belongs to the buyer.

Step 1 Calculate the number of days in the period.

$$31 \text{ days in July} - 14 \text{ days not counted} = 17 \text{ days counted}$$

$$14 \text{ days in August} + 17 \text{ days in July} = 31 \text{ days in period}$$

Step 2 Calculate the rent per day.

$$\$890 \div 31 \text{ days} = \$28.709677 \text{ per day}$$

$$\text{July 15 through July 27 used seller days} = 13 \text{ seller used days}$$

$$31 \text{ days in period} - 13 \text{ used days} = 18 \text{ unused days due buyer}$$

$$\$28.709677 \times 18 \text{ days} = \$516.77 \text{ (rounded) debit seller; credit buyer}$$

PRACTICE PROBLEMS

12. The sale of a duplex will close on December 12. The seller collected the rent for December, amounting to $548, on December 1. Day of closing belongs to the buyer. How should the rent be prorated on the closing statement? Who is debited and credited and for how much?

Debit the _____ $ _____

Credit the _____ $ _____

PRACTICE PROBLEMS

13. The sale of an apartment complex is scheduled to close on February 14. The complex contains five units, which rent for $650 per unit. The seller is also holding security deposits in the amount of $500 per unit. Day of closing belongs to the seller. How should the rent be prorated on the closing statement? Who will be debited and credited and for how much?

Debit the _____ $ _____

Credit the _____ $ _____

PRORATING MORTGAGE INTEREST

Because mortgage payments are normally paid each month, one month is usually the period used to calculate interest owed. Unless otherwise stated, mortgage interest is paid at the end of the period (in arrears), *or after* having use of the money. It is therefore charged to the seller up to the date of closing.

Mortgage interest is prorated in the same manner as property taxes. Interest is figured from the last date for which interest was paid. Unless stated otherwise, the exact number of days in each month is used, and interest is figured on a daily basis. Thus, the seller is *debited* (charged) up to midnight prior to the closing date and the buyer is *credited* for that period, with the buyer being responsible for the closing date and thereafter.

When solving problems dealing with interest in arrears, first determine the correct number of days allocated to the seller. Then convert those days into dollars and, unless directed otherwise, debit the seller and credit the buyer.

Example: A $130,000 mortgage is being assumed as of November 11 and interest for the month is $780. (The day of closing belongs to the buyer.)

Step 1 Divide the interest by 30 days to determine the mortgage interest per day

$780 ÷ 30 days = $26 per day

Step 2 Multiply the interest per day by the number of days the seller is charged. (Mortgage interest is paid in arrears, so we must charge the seller with the days used.)

The seller is charged from the first of the month through midnight of November 10.

$26 per day × 10 days = $260

This information would be entered on the closing statement as a $260 *debit* to the seller and a $260 *credit* to the buyer.

PRACTICE PROBLEMS

14. A $145,000 mortgage is assumed as of December 10. Interest for the month is $890. Prorate the mortgage interest. Charge the day of closing to the seller.

When the amount of interest must be determined before the interest can be prorated, use the following formula:

FORMULA

Prorated Interest

Mortgage balance × Annual interest rate = Annual interest

Annual interest ÷ 365 = Daily interest

Daily interest × Days interest is owed = Prorated interest

Example: A closing is scheduled for March 20. The buyer will assume the seller's existing mortgage of $63,500 at 5 percent interest, which is paid up to and including February 25. The next mortgage payment is due March 26. How will the mortgage interest be prorated on the closing statement? The buyer will pay the interest on the closing day.

Step 1   Calculate the number of days in the period.

Days in month (February 26 through March 25)

February 26 to March 1 = 3 days

March 1 to March 26 = 25 days

3 + 25 = 28 days of interest

Step 2   Calculate the number of days interest owed by seller.

February 26 to March 1 = 3 days

March 1 to March 20 = 19 days

3 + 19 = 22 days of interest owed by seller

Step 3   Calculate the annual interest and then the daily interest.

$63,500 \times 5\%$ = $3,175 annual interest

$3,175 \div 365$ = $8.6986301 daily interest

8.6986301×22 days = $191.37 (*debit* seller, *credit* buyer)

Note: When prorating interest that has been paid in advance by the seller, use the number of days the buyer will own the property and calculate this proration in the same way as interest paid in arrears. This amount results in a debit to the buyer and a credit to the seller.

PRACTICE PROBLEMS

15. The sale of a house is to be closed on August 12. The buyer will assume the existing mortgage of $40,000 at 5¾ percent interest. The buyer is to make the next payment on September 1. The last payment made by the seller paid the interest up to but not including August 1. Day of closing belongs to the buyer. How should the mortgage interest be prorated on the closing statement?

Debit the _____ $ _____

Credit the _____ $ _____

Using the information from this and previous chapters, solve the following problems (assume a 365-day year, day of closing belongs to the buyer, and use the tax rates provided on the Work Organizer for Closing Statements on page 144).

You sold a house for $80,000. The buyer made an earnest money deposit of $5,000 and will assume an existing FHA mortgage with an unpaid balance of $50,000 at 6½ percent interest. The seller has agreed to take back a new second mortgage of $15,000 with the remainder of the purchase price to be paid at closing, scheduled for May 16. The buyer is to pay the taxes associated with the assumed mortgage and the second mortgage. The seller is to pay the taxes associated with the deed. The property has been rented during the past year, and advance rent of $480 was collected by the seller for the month of May. Property taxes have been estimated at $1,095 for the year. The last payment made on the mortgage paid the interest up to and including April 30.

Prorations	Buyer/Seller		Amount
16. Taxes	Debit _____	Credit _____	$ _____
17. Rent	Debit _____	Credit _____	$ _____
18. Interest	Debit _____	Credit _____	$ _____

Expenses	Debit Buyer/Seller	Amount
19. Documentary stamps (deed)	_____	$ _____
20. Documentary stamps (note)	_____	$ _____
21. Intangible tax (mortgage)	_____	$ _____

Mr. Hernando has signed a purchase contract to buy a small rental duplex. The purchase price is $110,000, with the closing set for June 10. Mr. Hernando will assume the seller's mortgage, which has an unpaid balance of $70,300. The seller, Ms. Clay, has agreed to take back a new second mortgage in the amount of $28,000 with Mr. Hernando to pay the taxes related to the new and assumed mortgages. Ms. Clay will pay the taxes on the deed (use the tax rates provided on the Work Organizer for Closing Statements on page 144). Day of closing belongs to the buyer. Other contractual agreements (a 365-day year applies) are as follows:

> Binder deposit: $11,700.
>
> First mortgage interest: $565.50 in arrears (for the period June 1 through 30).
>
> Property taxes: city, school, district, and county taxes combined are estimated to be $3,294 for the year.
>
> Total rent: $1,710 collected in advance for the period June 1 through 30.
>
> Deed: warranty deed to be delivered with all required stamps paid.

Prorations	Buyer/Seller		Amount
22. Taxes	Debit _____	Credit _____	$ _____
23. Rent	Debit _____	Credit _____	$ _____
24. Interest	Debit _____	Credit _____	$ _____

Expenses	Debit Buyer/Seller	Amount
25. Documentary stamps (deed)	_____	$ _____
26. Documentary stamps (deed)	_____	$ _____
27. Intangible tax (mortgage)	_____	$ _____

PREPARING THE COMPOSITE CLOSING STATEMENT

To compute the individual amounts that are entered on a closing statement, a considerable number of calculations must be made. It is a good idea to use some type of worksheet to collect and organize the results of these computations. For this purpose, a Work Organizer for Closing Statements worksheet is provided at the end of this chapter. As individual results are computed in the lower portions of the form, they may be written in the appropriate space(s) in the upper portions for subsequent use.

Begin by carefully reading the closing statement problem and determining what information will need to be entered on the Work Organizer.

1. **Purchase price**—Enter the purchase price in the column labeled *Debit Buyer.* Also enter the price in the column labeled *Credit Seller.*

2. **Binder deposit**—The deposit is credited towards what the buyer owes and therefore is entered in the *Credit Buyer* column. The binder deposit is not entered on the seller side of the work organizer because the seller has not received the deposit (it has been held in the broker's or attorney's escrow account).

3. **Prorations**—Use the boxes on the lower half of the work organizer for calculating the applicable prorations. City and county property taxes may be calculated separately or lumped into a single proration. Remember, property taxes are normally paid in arrears, so you are concerned with the number of days of seller ownership. Calculate the amount the seller owes the buyer. The prorated amount is entered in the *Debit Seller* column. The same figure is also entered in the *Credit Buyer* column. If the property is an income-producing property, the prepaid rent must be prorated. Remember that the seller typically has received the rent at the beginning of the month. Therefore, you must calculate how many days of rent the buyer is entitled to receive in the month that the closing occurs. The prorated rent is entered in the *Credit Buyer* column. The same figure is also entered in the *Debit Seller* column. Lastly, check to see if the buyer is assuming the seller's mortgage. If so, you need to prorate the mortgage interest. Mortgage payments are typically paid in arrears. Therefore, you are concerned with the days of seller ownership. The prorated amount is entered in the *Debit Seller* column. The same figure is also entered in the *Credit Buyer* column.

4. **Documentary stamp taxes**—Use the boxes on the bottom row of the work organizer for calculating the applicable prorations. The seller typically is responsible for paying the documentary stamp tax on the deed. Doc stamps are a single-entry expense item. Enter the amount in the *Debit Seller* column. The buyer typically pays for the documentary stamp tax associated with financing the purchase. Enter documentary stamps on the note and intangible taxes, if applicable, in the *Debit Buyer* column. (*Note:* the fees listed in the bottom row of the work organizer may or may not be applicable in your state.)

5. **Other expenses**—Enter other expenses as a debit to the party responsible for the expense. Enter brokerage commission, attorney's fees, recording fees, and title insurance expenses in the appropriate party's debit column.

6. Note that the only item entered in the *Credit Seller* column of the work organizer is the purchase price. (If the seller prepaid any items, those items would also be entered in the *Credit Seller* column.)

7. If the seller is paying off an existing mortgage, the balance due is entered in the *Debit Seller* column of the work organizer. If the seller agrees to hold a newly created mortgage for part of the purchase price (purchase money mortgage) it would be entered in the *Debit Seller* column because the seller's cash at closing must be reduced by the amount of the seller financing. As mentioned earlier, the seller's portion of applicable prorated property taxes,

mortgage interest, and advance rent is entered in the *Debit Seller* column. If the property is rental property, security deposits held by the seller are entered in the *Debit Seller* column. Expenses entered in the *Debit Seller* column typically include the broker's commission, owner's title insurance, expense for preparing the deed, and the seller's attorney's fee.

8. Items that are entered in the *Credit Buyer* column include the earnest money deposit and any existing mortgages that the buyer is assuming, if applicable. New financing secured by the buyer is entered in the *Credit Buyer* column. As mentioned earlier, prorated property taxes, unpaid mortgage interest on an assumed mortgage, and prepaid rent are entered in the *Credit Buyer* column. Lastly, any tenant security deposits are entered in the *Credit Buyer* column of the work organizer.

9. Items that are entered in the *Debit Buyer* column include the lender's title insurance policy, state documentary stamp taxes on the note and intangible taxes, if applicable, and as mentioned earlier, the purchase price. Typical buyer expenses entered in the *Debit Buyer* column include the fee for recording the deed and the mortgage, if applicable, buyer's attorney's fees, and the fees association with preparing the mortgage and note.

When the time to prepare a formal closing statement arrives (see the Composite Closing Statement form), transfer the figures from the work organizer to the Composite Closing Statement.

FIVE PARTS TO THE COMPOSITE CLOSING STATEMENT

The Composite Closing Statement is so named because the entire transaction is entered on a single form. The Composite Closing Statement consists of a seller's statement, a buyer's statement, and a broker's statement. There are five main parts to the Composite Closing Statement.

1. **Information section**—Enter the purchase price, the binder deposit, and any mortgages involved in the transaction.

2. **Proration section**—Enter each prorated expense. Recall that a proration is a double entry. One party is debited and the other party is credited. Items that typically are entered in this section are property taxes, interest on assumed mortgages, and rents collect in advance by the seller.

3. **Expenses section**—Each expense is entered in this section. Expenses are entered as a debit to the party charged for the expense. Typical expenses include the brokerage commission, documentary stamp taxes, attorney's fees, title insurance, and the survey.

4. **Summation section**—In this section each column is totaled. There are four columns to total: the *Seller's Debits*, *Seller's Credits*, *Buyer's Debits*, and *Buyer's Credits*. Then, on the seller's side of the statement, the *Total Debits* are subtracted from the *Total Credits* to determine the balance due the seller. On the buyer's side of the statement, the credits are subtracted from the debits to determine the balance owed by the buyer.

5. **Broker's statement**—This statement is prepared to assure the broker that the escrow account will remain in balance after the closing. Cash receipts are entered in one column and cash disbursements are entered in the other column. The sum of each column must match.

Work Organizer for Closing Statements

Debit Buyer	Credit Buyer	Debit Seller	Credit Seller
Purchase	Deposit $ _____	1st Mortgage $ _____	Purchase
Price $ _____	1st Mortgage _____	2nd Mortgage _____	Price $ _____
	2nd Mortgage _____	Doc. Stamps	
	Prorated:	on Deed _____	
1st Mortgage _____	City Taxes _____	Title Insurance _____	1st Mortgage _____
2nd Mortgage _____	County Taxes _____	Intang. Tax	2nd Mortgage _____
Doc. Stamps	Rent _____	on Mortgage $ _____	
1st Note _____	Mort. Int. _____	Prorated:	
2nd Note _____	Security	City taxes _____	
	Deposit _____	County Taxes	
Intang. Tax	TOTAL CREDITS $ _____	Rent _____	TOTAL CREDITS $ _____
on Mortgage _____		Mort. Interest _____	
	– – – – – – – – –	Atty. Fees _____	– – – – – – – – –
Atty. Fees _____	Total Debits $ _____		Total Credits $ _____
Record Deed _____	less	Commission _____	less
Record Mort. _____	Total Credits $ _____	Miscellaneous _____	Total Debits $ _____
Title Ins. _____			
TOTAL BUYER	DUE FROM	TOTAL SELLER	BALANCE DUE
DEBITS $ _____	BUYER $ _____	DEBITS $ _____	SELLER $ _____

CITY TAXES	COUNTY TAXES	PREPAID RENT
Annual taxes ÷ 365 = daily cost	Annual taxes ÷ 365 = daily cost	Amt./period ÷ days in period
Daily cost × no. of days used by Seller	Daily cost × no. of days used by Seller	Days owned by Buyer _____ ×
(DEBIT SELLER; CREDIT BUYER)	(DEBIT SELLER; CREDIT BUYER)	amount per day _____
		(DEBIT SELLER; CREDIT BUYER)

1st MORTGAGE INTEREST	1st MORTGAGE INTEREST	COMMISSION
Balance due × % = annual int.	Balance due × % = annual int.	Purchase price
Annual int. ÷ 365 = daily int.	Annual int. ÷ 365 = daily int.	$_____ × _____%
Daily int. × no. of days used	Daily int. × no. of days used	

DOC. STAMPS DEED	DOC. STAMPS NOTE	INTAGE. TAX MORT.	MISCELLANEOUS
$ .70 × $100 on purchase price	$ .35 × $100 on note face value	.002 mills × $1 mortgage face value	

For practice, use the actual tax rates in effect for your state.

Note: The debiting/crediting of all items may vary and is negotiable

Closing date: Month _____ Day _____ Year _____ ("charged" to_____

Method of prorating: _____

COMPOSITE CLOSING STATEMENT

SELLER'S STATEMENT			BUYER'S STATEMENT	
Debit	Credit	Item	Debit	Credit
		Purchase Terms:		
		Total purchase price		
		Binder deposit		
		First mortgage – balance		
		Second mortgage		
		Prorations & Prepayments:		
		Rent		
		Interest – first mortgage		
		Interest – second mortgage		
		Prepaid – first mortgage		
		Prepaid – second mortgage		
		Taxes – city		
		Taxes – county		
		Other:		
		Expenses:		
		Attorney's fees		
		Title insurance		
		Brokerage commission		
		Documentary Stamps:		
		State tax on deed		
		State tax on note		
		State intangible tax on mortgage		
		Recording:		
		Mortgage		
		Deed		
		Miscellaneous:		
		TOTAL – DEBITS & CREDITS		
	BALANCE DUE TO SELLER	BALANCE DUE FROM BUYER		
		GRAND TOTALS		

BROKER'S STATEMENT

	Receipts	Disbursements
Binder deposit	_____	_____
Check from buyer at closing	_____	_____
Brokerage commission	_____	_____
Check to seller at closing	_____	_____
Seller's expense (less brokerage)	_____	_____
Buyer's expense	_____	_____
TOTALS:	_____	_____

ANSWER KEY

1. $930 rent per month ÷ 30 days = $31 rent per day

2. 30 days – 9 used days = 21 unused days owed the buyer

3. $31 daily rent rate × 21 days = $651 proration

4. Months: Jan., Feb., Mar., and Apr.; 30 + 30 + 30 + 19 = 109 days

5. $3,600 annual cost ÷ 360 = $10 daily cost; $10 × 109 days = $1,090

6. Months: Jan., Feb., and Mar.; Days: 31 + 28 + 6 = 65 days

7. Months: Jan., Feb., Mar., Apr., May, and June; Days: 31 + 28 + 31 + 30 + 31 + 30 = 181 days; 181 days + 11 days in December + 29 days in July = 221 days

8. Months: Apr., May, June, and July; Days: 30 + 31 + 30 + 31 = 122 days; 122 days + 28 days in March + 17 days in August = 167 days

9. Months: Jan., Feb., Mar., Apr., May, June, July, Aug., and Sept.; Days: 31 + 28 + 31 + 30 + 31 + 30 + 31 + 31 + 30 = 273 days; 273 + 15 days in October = 288 days; $876 ÷ 365 = $2.40 per day; 288 × $2.40 = $691.20 (debit seller, credit buyer)

10. Months: Jan., Feb., Mar., Apr., May, June, July, and Aug.; Days: 30 × 8 = 240 days + 16 = 256 days; $1,876 ÷ 360 = $5.2111; $5.2111 × 256 = $1,334.04 (debit seller, credit buyer)

11. $360 rent per unit × 5 units = $1,800 total monthly rent; 30 days in month – 20 days used portion = 10 days owed buyer; $1,800 ÷ 30 days × 10 days = $600 (debit seller, credit buyer)

12. $548 ÷ 31 = $17.677419; 31 days – 11 days used = 20 unused days owed buyer; 20 days × $17.677419 = $353.55 (debit seller, credit buyer)

13. $650 rent × 5 units = $3,250 total monthly rent; $3,250 ÷ 28 days = $116.07143 daily rent; 28 days in February – 14 seller days = 14 unused days owed buyer; $116.07143 × 14 days = $1,625 rent due buyer; $500 × 5 units = $2,500 security deposits; $2,500 security deposits + $1,625 rent = $4,125 prorated amount (debit seller, credit buyer)

14. $890 monthly interest ÷ 31 days = $28.709678 interest per day; $29.709678 × 10 days owed by seller = $287.10 (debit seller, credit buyer)

15. $40,000 × .0575 = $2,300 annual interest; $2,300 ÷ 365 = $6.30137 daily interest; 11 days in August × $6.30137 = $69.32 (debit seller, credit buyer)

16. Months: Jan., Feb., Mar., Apr., and May; Days: 31 + 28 + 31 + 30 + 15 = 135 days; $1,095 ÷ 365 × 135 = $405; Taxes are paid in arrears, therefore, debit seller $405, credit buyer $405

17. $480 ÷ 31 × 16 = $247.74; Seller has already collected the rent, therefore, debit seller $247.74, credit buyer $247.74

18. $50,000 × .065 = $3,250; $3,250 ÷ 365 = $8.90411 × 15 = $133.56; Debit seller $133.56, credit buyer $133.56

19. $80,000 ÷ 100 = 800 tax increments; 800 × $.70 = $560 debit to seller

20. $15,000 ÷ 100 = 150 tax increments; 150 × $.35 = $52.50; $50,000 ÷ 100 = 500 tax increments; 500 × $.35 = $175; $175 + $52.50 = $227.50 debit to buyer

21. $15,000 × .002 = $30

22. Months: Jan., Feb., Mar., Apr., May, and June; Days: 31 + 28 + 31 + 30 + 31 + 9 = 160 days; $3,294 ÷ 365 × 160 = $1,443.95; Taxes are paid in arrears, therefore, debit seller $1,443.95, credit buyer $1,443.95

23. $1,710 ÷ 30 × 21 days = $1,197; Seller has already collected the rent, therefore, debit seller $1,197, credit buyer $1,197

24. $565.50 ÷ 30 × 9 = $169.65;
Interest is paid in arrears, therefore, debit seller
$169.65, credit buyer $169.65

25. $110,000 ÷ 100 = 1,100 tax increments;
1,100 × $.70 = $770; Debit seller $770

26. $28,000 ÷ 100 = 280 tax increments;
280 × $.35 = $98.00;
$70,300 ÷ 100 = 703 tax increments;
703 × $.35 = $246.05;
$246.05 + $98 = $344.05;
Debit buyer $344.05

27. $28,000 × $.002 = $56;
Debit buyer $56

P o s t | Test I

The following three practice examinations are representative of the type of math problems that may appear on your license exam. Posttest III includes math problems for broker candidates. However, the closing statement problems are appropriate for all exam candidates. The math calculations have all been explained in this book. Each test question is cross-referenced to the chapter where you will find a detailed explanation of the particular calculation.

1. Calculate the selling price of a home with selling expenses of 4 percent of the sale price, an outstanding mortgage balance of $84,780, and net proceeds to the seller of $9,970. (Chapter 3)

   a. $91,105.77
   b. $98,141.20
   c. $98,282.50
   d. $98,697.92

2. A parcel of land measures 180 feet by 250 feet. How many acres does the parcel contain? (Chapter 4)

   a. 0.97
   b. 1.03
   c. 1.20
   d. 1.23

3. Your business records reveal that it takes you an average of 10 showings to sell a house. You have analyzed your expenses to show houses and have found that $25 is the average cost to show a house one time. Your broker retains 40 percent of the 7 percent sale commission charged for selling residential properties. If you sell a house for $116,000, what is your net pre-tax income from the sale? (Chapter 3)

   a. $2,998
   b. $3,248
   c. $4,622
   d. $4,872

4. The monthly payment for principal and interest on a $64,500 loan at 8½ percent for 30 years is $495.95. What amount of the second month's payment will be applied to principal? (Chapter 5)

   a. $39.07
   b. $39.35
   c. $456.59
   d. $456.88

5. The street in front of your house is to be paved at a cost of $35 per foot of frontage. The city has agreed to pay 30 percent of the paving cost and will assess abutting properties for the remainder. If your frontage on that street is 75 feet, what will be your portion of the special assessment? (Chapter 6)

   a. $787.50
   b. $918.75
   c. $1,837.50
   d. $2,625

6. At the expiration of a loan period of 18 months, a broker paid his bank a total of $20,565, which included $2,565 interest. What was the simple interest rate? (Chapter 5)

   a. 8.32%
   b. 8.50%
   c. 9.07%
   d. 9.50%

7. A developer purchased two 115-foot lots for $23,500 net each and divided them into three lots of equal front footage. The developer sold the lots for $225 per front foot. What is the developer's percentage of profit? (Chapter 2)

   a. 9%
   b. 9.18%
   c. 9.75%
   d. 10.11%

8. Calculate the number of acres contained in the following legal description: "The NE¼ of the SE¼ and the SE¼ of the NE¼ and the N½ of the NE¼." (Chapter 4)

   a. 30 acres
   b. 80 acres
   c. 120 acres
   d. 160 acres

9. Last year a homeowner paid $3,054 in property taxes on property with a total taxable value of $116,030. What was the tax rate in mills? (Round to the nearest tenth of a mill.) (Chapter 6)

   a. 1.1 mills
   b. 2.6 mills
   c. 26.3 mills
   d. 33.5 mills

10. A warehouse unit is 15 feet by 30 feet and rents for $720 per month. Calculate the annual rental income per square foot. (Chapter 4)

   a. $19.20
   b. $28.50
   c. $32.10
   d. $37.04

11. A real estate investor has $150,000 to invest in income-producing property. She is looking for a first-year return of 15 percent on her money. What must a property produce as first-year net income to attract this investor? (Chapter 7)

   a. $10,000
   b. $15,000
   c. $22,500
   d. $23,000

12. A two-story home contains 850 square feet of living area on each floor. The home also features a 20 × 24 foot garage. The reproduction cost new of the living area is $95 per square foot and $52.50 per square foot for the garage. What is the reproduction cost new of the structure? (Chapter 7)

   a. $80,750
   b. $105,900
   c. $161,500
   d. $186,700

13. A small apartment building contains three apartments that are all leased and occupied. Apartment 1 is 32' × 35½' and rents for $3,960 per year; apartment 2 is 30' × 40' and rents for $300 per month; and apartment 3 is 24' × 36' and rents for $70 per week. What is the average annual income per square foot? (Chapter 4)

   a. $2.25
   b. $2.47
   c. $2.63
   d. $3.50

14. A buyer is approved for a 70 percent loan on a purchase price of $116,000. The buyer has paid a $5,000 earnest money deposit. How much additional cash must the buyer provide at closing? (Chapter 5)

   a. $3,867
   b. $29,800
   c. $34,800
   d. $76,200

15. A contractor borrowed $38,000 at 10 percent simple interest on a 30-month term loan. At the end of the period, he paid back the borrowed amount plus all interest in one payment. What amount was the single payment? (Chapter 5)

   a. $9,500
   b. $41,800
   c. $47,500
   d. $48,200

16. What is the monthly gross rent multiplier for a house that sold for $97,900 and rents for $890 per month? (Chapter 7)

   a. 90
   b. 110
   c. 120
   d. 150

Use the following information to answer problems 17 and 18:

A home sold for $96,700 with 30-year, fixed-rate financing at 7½ percent interest. The mortgage discount was 3 points. The property was assessed at 95 percent of the sale price, and the total ad valorem tax rate was 29 mills.

17. Calculate the lender's approximate yield. (Chapter 5)

    a. 7½%
    b. 7¾%
    c. 7⅞%
    d. 8%

18. Calculate the annual property taxes. (Chapter 6)

    a. $2,003.00
    b. $2,113.09
    c. $2,160.47
    d. $2,664.09

Use the following information to answer problems 19 and 20:

A couple purchase a home for $116,000 and secure a new nonqualifying mortgage with a 30 percent cash down payment.

19. Calculate the documentary stamp tax on the deed based on a tax rate of $.70 per $100. (Chapter 6)

    a. $371.20
    b. $580
    c. $696
    d. $812

20. Calculate the intangible tax associated with the new mortgage based on a tax rate of 2 mills. (Chapter 5)

    a. $162.40
    b. $232.40
    c. $371.20
    d. $568.40

POSTTEST I ANSWER KEY

1. d. $98,697.92
    $84,780 loan + $9,970 seller proceeds = $94,750
    $94,750 (part) ÷ .96 (rate) = $98,697.92 (total)

2. b. 1.03
    180 feet × 250 feet = 45,000 square feet
    45,000 square feet ÷ 43,560 square feet per acre = 1.03 acres

3. c. $4,622
    $25 average cost to show × 10 = $250 cost per sale
    $116,000 sale price × .07 = $8,120 commission
    $8,120 × .60 = $4,872
    $4,872 – $250 expenses of sale =
    $4,622 net pre-tax income

4. b. $39.35
    $64,500 loan × .085 interest rate =
    $5,482.50 interest; $5,482.50 ÷ 12 months =
    $456.88 interest, month one
    $495.95 – $456.88 =
    $39.07 principal paid, month one
    $64,500 – $39.07=
    $64,460.93 remaining loan balance
    $64,460.93 × .085 = $5,479.18 interest
    $5,479.18 ÷ 12 months =
    $456.60 interest, month two
    $495.95 – $456.60 = $39.35 principal paid, month two

5. b. $918.75
    75 feet × $35 = $2,625 total cost
    $2,625 × .70 = $1,837.50, property owner's share
    $1,837.50 ÷ 2 = $918.75, your portion

6. d. 9.5%
    $2,565 interest ÷ 18 months = $142.50 per month
    × 12 months = $1,710 interest/year
    $20,565 – $2,565 = $18,000 principal
    $1,710 ÷ $18,000 = 9.5% interest rate

7. d. 10.11%
    $23,500 × 2 lots = $47,000 paid
    115 front feet × 2 lots = 230 front feet
    230 front feet × $225 = $51,750 selling price
    $51,750 – $47,000 = $4,750 profit
    $4,750 ÷ $47,000 = 10.11% percentage of profit

8. d. 160
    640 acres ÷ 4 ÷ 2 = 80 acres
    640 acres ÷ 4 ÷ 4 = 40 acres
    640 acres ÷ 4 ÷ 4 = 40 acres
    80 + 40 + 40 = 160 acres

9. c. 26.3
    $3,054 property taxes ÷ $116,030 taxable value = .0263208
    .0263208 = 26.3 mills (rounded to the nearest tenth of a mill)

10. *a.* $19.20

15 feet × 30 feet = 450 square feet

$720 × 12 months = $8,640 rent per year

$8,640 ÷ 450 square feet = $19.20 per square foot

11. *c.* $22,500

$150,000 × .15 = $22,500 net income

12. *d.* $186,700

850 square feet × 2 stories = 1,700 total square feet of living area

1,700 square feet × $95 = $161,500 reproduction cost new of living area

20' × 24' = 480 square feet of garage

480 square feet × $52.50 = $25,200 reproduction cost new of garage

$161,500 + $25,200 = $186,700 total reproduction cost new

13. *d.* $3.50

32' × 35.5' = 1,136 square feet in apartment 1 at $3,960 annual rent

30' × 40' = 1,200 square feet in apartment 2 at $300 × 12 months = $3,600 annual rent

24' × 36' = 864 square feet in apartment 3 at $70 × 52 weeks = $3,640 annual rent

$3,960 + $3,600 + $3,640 = $11,200 total annual rent

1,136 square feet + 1,200 square feet + 864 square feet = 3,200 total square footage

$11,200 ÷ 3,200 square feet = $3.50 annual income per square foot

14. *b.* $29,800

$116,000 sale price × .30 down = $34,800 down payment

$34,800 – $5,000 = $29,800 balance due at closing

15. *c.* $47,500

$38,000 loan × .10 interest = $3,800

$3,800 ÷ 12 months = $316.67 interest per month

$316.67 × 30 months = $9,500 total interest

$9,500 + $38,000 = $47,500

16. *b.* 110

$97,900 sale price ÷ $890 rent = 110 GRM

17. *c.* 7⅞%

7½% = 7⁴⁄₈%

⅜% + 7⁴⁄₈% = 7⅞%

18. *d.* $2,664.09

$96,700 sale price × .95 = $91,865 assessed value

$91,865 × .029 mills = $2,664.09 property tax

19. *d.* $812

$116,000 ÷ $100 increments = 1,160 taxable increments

1,160 × $.70 = $812

20. *a.* $162.40

$116,000 × .70 = $81,200

$81,200 × $.002 = $162.40

1. The NW¼ of the NE¼ of the SW¼, Section 20, Township 4 South, Range 2 East, describes a tract of _____ (Chapter 4)

   a. .125 acre.
   b. .5 acre.
   c. 10 acres.
   d. 64 acres.

2. A buyer has made an earnest money deposit of $10,150 on a house selling for $94,500. A local thrift institution has agreed to lend 85 percent of the selling price at 6½ percent interest for 30 years. If the buyer's closing costs amount to $1,575, how much more cash must the buyer produce at closing? (Chapter 5)

   a. $5,600
   b. $7,175
   c. $12,889
   d. $14,175

3. An undeveloped tract of land has 2,080 feet of highway frontage with a perpendicular boundary measuring 2,095 feet. The property is triangular-shaped and has been sold for $4,000 per acre. Rounding the tract acreage to the nearest acre, the sale price is _____ (Chapter 4)

   a. $50,000.
   b. $100,000.
   c. $200,000.
   d. $400,000.

4. A builder borrowed $72,000 to build a house. He agreed to pay $2,160 per quarter in interest until the house was sold. From the sale of the house, he is to pay the entire loan principal in one lump sum. The annual interest rate of the loan is _____ (Chapter 5)

   a. 6 percent.
   b. 9 percent.
   c. 12 percent.
   d. 15 percent.

Use the following information to answer problems 5 and 6:

A farmer decides to lease part of his land. He agrees to an annual lease rate of $150 per acre to be paid for tillable land only. The leased tract measures 600' × 1,815' and has a required drainage pond within its boundaries. The drainage pond is 120 feet wide and 726 feet long.

5. How many acres of tillable land are available for lease? (Chapter 4)

   a. 23
   b. 25
   c. 27
   d. 30

6. What amount will the farmer receive under the terms cited? (Chapter 3)

   a. $2,875
   b. $3,450
   c. $3,750
   d. $4,500

7. A mortgage contract requires monthly payments of $500. The first month's interest amounted to $400, with the balance of the monthly payment applied to reduction of principal. If the annual rate of interest is 10 percent, what was the original amount of the loan? (Chapters 3 and 5)

   a. $40,000
   b. $48,000
   c. $53,333
   d. $60,000

Use the following information to answer problems 8 through 10:

A brokerage firm lists a small office building for $225,000. The broker agrees to a graduated sale commission rate of 5 percent on the first $50,000 of the sale price, 6 percent on the next $100,000, and 10 percent of any balance. A sales associate sold the property for $220,000. From the total sale commission received, the broker paid the listing sales associate 20 percent and divided the remainder of the sale commission evenly between himself and the sales associate who sold the property.

8. What was the total sale commission received by the brokerage firm? (Chapter 3)

   a. $12,700
   b. $15,500
   c. $16,000
   d. $19,500

9. What amount did the listing sales associate receive? (Chapter 3)

   a. $1,550
   b. $3,100
   c. $7,750
   d. $12,400

10. What amount did the selling sales associate receive? (Chapter 3)

    a. $3,100
    b. $4,650
    c. $6,200
    d. $7,750

11. A lender requires a yield of 7½ percent interest, but has quoted an interest rate of 6¼ percent. How many points must the lender charge to obtain the required yield? (Chapter 5)

    a. 4 points
    b. 6 points
    c. 8 points
    d. 10 points

12. A couple has a combined gross monthly income of $6,500. They have applied for a VA loan of $230,000 at 6½ percent interest for 30 years. Monthly payments of principal and interest total $1,453.76. Annual property taxes are $1,800 and their property insurance is $1,200 per year. They have a monthly car payment of $425. What is their total obligations ratio? (Chapter 5)

    a. 26.2%
    b. 28.9%
    c. 32.8%
    d. 41%

13. The city tax rate is 9.25 mills, the county tax rate is 8.5 mills and the school board tax rate is 5.5 mills. A home is valued at $350,000 and is located within the city limits. The home is assessed at 85 percent of value. The homeowner qualifies for a $25,000 homestead exemption. What is the cost of the property taxes? (Chapter 6)

    a. $6,335.63
    b. $6,823.54
    c. $6,916.88
    d. $7,556.25

14. The seller wants to net $150,000. Seller closing costs are estimated at $5,000. The broker charges a 6 percent commission. What must the property sell for? (Round to the nearest even $100.) (Chapter 3)

    a. $159,000
    b. $164,000
    c. $164,900
    d. $165,230

15. A house contains 1,500 square feet. The lot is valued at $17,100. What is the cost to reproduce the house new if an accrued depreciation of 4 percent was applied to determine the house's current appraised value of $81,792? (Chapter 7)

    a. $78,520
    b. $85,200
    c. $94,936
    d. $103,013

16. A lease calls for monthly minimum rent of $700 plus 3½ percent of annual gross sales in excess of $200,000. What was the annual rent for the year if the annual gross sales were $300,000? (Chapter 7)

    a. $4,200

    b. $6,820

    c. $10,500

    d. $11,900

Use the following information for problems 17 through 19:

An FHA appraiser has appraised a house at $68,000. The buyer has found a lender willing to finance the purchase of the house with an FHA mortgage at 7½ percent interest. A discount of 4 points will be required to conclude the financing.

17. What is the borrower's minimum cash investment for this loan? (Chapter 5)

    a. $3,900

    b. $3,400

    c. $2,900

    d. $2,040

18. What is the cost of the mortgage discount points? (Round to nearest $1.) (Chapter 5)

    a. $2,500

    b. $2,638

    c. $2,659

    d. $2,720

19. The lender's approximate yield is _____ (Chapter 5)

    a. 7.5 percent.

    b. 7.9 percent.

    c. 8.0 percent.

    d. 11.5 percent.

20. A house sold for $117,800. If the sales associate received $4,123 as a commission for selling the house, what percent of the sale price was her commission? (Chapter 3)

    a. 3½%

    b. 4.6%

    c. 5%

    d. 7%

POSTTEST II ANSWER KEY

1. *c.* 10

640 acres ÷ 4 ÷ 4 ÷ 4 = 10 acres

2. *a.* $5,600

$94,500 sale price × .15 down =
$14,175 down payment
$14,175 + $1,575 buyer closing costs = $15,750
$15,750 – $10,150 = $5,600 balance due at closng

3. *c.* $200,000

Area = ½(base × height)
2,080' × 2,095' = 4,357,600 square feet
4,357,600 square feet ÷ 2 = 2,178,800 square feet
2,178,800 square feet ÷ 43,560 square feet per acre = 50.0184 or 50 acres
50 acres × $4,000 per acre = $200,000

4. *c.* .12 or 12%

$2,160 × 4 quarters = $8,640 interest/year
$8,640 ÷ $72,000 = .12 or 12% interest

5. *a.* 23

600' × 1,815' = 1,089,000 total square feet
120' × 726' = 87,120 square feet of pond
1,089,000 square feet – 87,120 square feet =
1,001,880 tillable square feet
1,001,880 square feet ÷ 43,560 square feet per acre = 23 acres

6. *b.* $3,450

$150 × 23 acres = $3,450

7. *b.* $48,000

$400 × 12 months = $4,800 interest/year
$4,800 (*part*) ÷ .10 (*rate*) = $48,000 loan (*total*)

8. *b.* $15,500

$50,000 × .05 = $2,500
$100,000 × .06 = $6,000
$220,000 – $150,000 = $70,000
$70,000 × .10 = $7,000
$2,500 + $6,000 + $7,000 = $15,500 total commission

9. *b.* $3,100

$15,500 total commission × .20 = $3,100 listing sales associate's commission

10. *c.* $6,200

$15,500 × .20 = $3,100 listing sales associate's commission
$15,500 − $3,100 = $12,400
$12,400 ÷ 2 = $6,200 selling sales associate's commission

11. *d.* 10

7.50% − 6.25% = 1.25% difference
1.25% ÷ .125% = 10 points

12. *c.* .3275 or 32.8%

$1,800 taxes ÷ 12 months = $150 per month
$1,200 insurance ÷ 12 months = $100 per month
$1,453.76 P&I + $150 taxes + $100 insurance + $425 car payment = $2,128.76 PITIO
$2,128.76 PITIO ÷ $6,500 gross monthly income = .3275 or 32.8%

13. *a.* $6,335.63

9.25 + 8.5 + 5.5 = 23.25 mills
$350,000 × .85 = $297,500 assessed value
$297,500 − $25,000 exemption = $272,500
$272,500 × .02325 = $6,335.63

14. *c.* $164,893.62 (round to $164,900)

$150,000 + $5,000 = $155,000 (*part*)
100% − 6% = 94% (*rate*)
$155,000 ÷ .94 = $164,893.62 (round to $164,900)

15. *b.* $85,200

$81,792 ÷ .96 = $85,200

16. *d.* $11,900

$300,000 − $200,000 = $100,000 subject to 3.5% charge
$100,000 × .035 = $3,500 additional rent
$700 × 12 = $8,400 annual base rent
$8,400 + $3,500 = $11,900 annual rent

17. *d.* $2,040

$68,000 × .03 =
$2,040 minimum cash investment

18. *b.* $2,638.40 (round to $2,638)

$68,000 × .9775 = $66,470 maximum FHA loan
$68,000 − $66,470 = $1,530 (does not meet minimum cash investment)
$68,000 − $2,040 minimum cash investment = $65,960 FHA loan amount
$65,960 × .04 = $2,638.40 cost of points (round to $2,638)

19. *c.* 8 percent

⅛% = .125%
.125% × 4 points = ⁴⁄₈% = .5%
7.5% + .5% = 8%

20. *a.* 3½%

$4,123 commission ÷ $117,800 sale price = .035;
.035 = 3.5% commission

P o s t | **Test III** (Broker Candidates)

Use the following information to answer problems 1 through 12:

An investor purchased an apartment building in January for $395,000. The contract specified that $75,000 of the purchase price was for the land and the balance was for the structure. The investor made a down payment of 10 percent and financed the remainder of the purchase. The mortgage is for 30 years at 7½ percent interest with a monthly payment of $2,485.71. The apartment building consists of 12 apartments that rent for $600 per month. Vacancy and collection losses are estimated at 6 percent. Operating expenses are 30 percent of the effective gross income and include reserves of $10,000.

1. What is the PGI for this property? (Chapter 7)
   a. $7,200
   b. $24,560
   c. $57,300
   d. $86,400

2. What is the EGI for this property? (Chapter 7)
   a. $6,768
   b. $57,300
   c. $81,216
   d. $86,400

3. What is the total operating expense for this property? (Round to the nearest dollar.) (Chapter 7)
   a. $25,920
   b. $24,365
   c. $14,365
   d. $6,400

4. What is the NOI for this property? (Chapter 7)
   a. $24,365
   b. $38,225
   c. $56,851
   d. $62,035

5. What is the annual debt service for this property? (Round to the nearest dollar.) (Chapter 7)
   a. $2,486
   b. $24,365
   c. $24,857
   d. $29,829

6. What is the debt service coverage ratio for this property? (Chapter 7)
   a. 1.91
   b. 1.97
   c. 2.10
   d. 2.33

7. What is the before-tax cash flow for this property? (Chapter 7)
   a. $27,022
   b. $29,829
   c. $32,486
   d. $54,365

8. What is the operating expense ratio for this property? (Chapter 7)
   a. 0.28
   b. 0.30
   c. 0.38
   d. 0.43

9. What is the equity dividend rate for this property? (Chapter 7)
   a. 32.3%
   b. 41.6%
   c. 53.5%
   d. 68.4%

10. What is the IRS depreciation allowance for this property? (Round to the nearest dollar.) (Chapter 7)
    a. $10,323
    b. $11,636
    c. $12,742
    d. $14,364

11. What is the cash break-even ratio for this propery? (Chapter 7)

   a. 51.2%
   b. 54.5%
   c. 62.7%
   d. 77.8%

12. What is the capitalization rate for this property? (Chapter 7)

   a. 0.12
   b. 0.14
   c. 0.15
   d. 0.18

Use the following information to answer problems 13 through 20:

   You sold a duplex for $143,500. The seller has agreed to a 6 percent sale commission. The closing is set for March 15. The buyer will assume the seller's FHA mortgage, which has an unpaid balance of $89,700. The seller has agreed to take back a new second mortgage in the amount of $25,000. The buyer will pay the taxes related to the financing. The seller will pay the taxes on the deed. Prorations are to be calculated using the 365-day method (day of closing belongs to the buyer). The buyer has paid a $10,000 earnest money deposit. Property taxes are estimated to be $4,325 for the year (and have not been paid). Rent was collected at the first of the month in the amount of $1,500 per unit. Monthly mortgage payments are paid in arrears. The first mortgage interest for the period March 1 through March 31 is $723.50.

13. Calculate the property tax proration. How will the information be entered on the closing statement? (Chapter 8)

   a. $865 debit seller; $865 credit buyer
   b. $876.85 credit seller; $876.85 debit buyer
   c. $865 credit buyer; $3,460 debit buyer
   d. $3,460 debit seller; $3,460 credit buyer

14. Calculate the rent proration. How will the information be entered on the closing statement? (Chapter 8)

   a. $822.58 debit seller; $822.58 credit buyer
   b. $1,354.84 debit buyer; $1,354.84 credit seller
   c. $1,645.16 debit seller; $1,645.16 credit buyer
   d. $1,700 debit seller; $1,300 credit buyer

15. Calculate the mortgage interest proration. How will the information be entered on the closing statement? (Chapter 8)

   a. $326.74 debit seller; $326.74 credit buyer
   b. $326.74 debit seller; $396.76 credit buyer
   c. $396.76 debit seller; $396.76 credit buyer
   d. $409.98 debit seller; $409.98 credit buyer

16. Calculate the documentary stamp tax on the deed based on a tax rate of $.70 per $100. How will the information be entered on the closing statement? (Chapter 6)

   a. $502.25 debit buyer
   b. $1,004.50 debit seller
   c. $200.90 debit seller; $200.90 credit buyer
   d. $502.25 debit seller; $502.25 credit buyer

17. Calculate the documentary stamp taxes on the note owed on this transaction based on a tax rate of $.35 per $100. (Chapter 5)

   a. $87.50 debit buyer
   b. $313.95 debit buyer
   c. $401.45 debit seller
   d. $401.45 debit buyer

18. Calculate the intangible taxes associated with this transaction based on a tax rate of 2 mills. How will the information be entered on the closing statement? (Chapter 5)

   a. $50 debit buyer
   b. $179.40 debit seller
   c. $229.40 debit seller; $229.40 credit buyer
   d. $500 debit buyer

19. How much additional down payment does the buyer owe at closing? (Chapter 8)

   a. $10,000
   b. $18,800
   c. $25,000
   d. $28,800

20. Calculate the sale commission. How will the commission be entered on the closing statement? (Chapters 3 and 8)

   a. $5,382 debit buyer
   b. $5,382 debit seller
   c. $8,610 debit buyer
   d. $8,610 debit seller

POSTTEST III ANSWER KEY

1. *d.* $86,400
   $600 rent × 12 apartments × 12 months = $86,400 PGI

2. *c.* $81,216
   $86,400 × .06 = $5,184 vacancy and collection losses
   $86,400 PGI – $5,184 = $81,216 EGI

3. *b.* $24,365
   $81,216 EGI × .30 = $24,364.80 operating expenses = $24,365 (rounded)

4. *c.* $56,851
   $81,216 EGI – $24,365 operating expenses = $56,851 NOI

5. *d.* $29,829
   $2,485.71 × 12 months = $29,828.52 annual debt service = $29,829 (rounded)

6. *a.* 1.91
   NOI ÷ annual debt service = debt service coverage ratio
   $56,851 NOI ÷ $29,829 debt service = 1.91 debt service coverage ratio

7. *a.* $27,022
   NOI – annual debt service = before-tax cash flow
   $56,851 NOI – $29,829 annual debt service = $27,022 before-tax cash flow

8. *b.* 0.30
   Operating expenses ÷ EGI = operating expense ratio
   $24,365 operating expenses ÷ $81,216 EGI = .30 operating expense ratio

9. *d.* 68.4%
   First year before-tax cash flow ÷ down payment = equity dividend rate
   $395,000 sale price × .10 = $39,500 down payment
   $27,022 first year before-tax cash flow ÷ $39,500 down payment = .684 or 68.4% equity dividend rate

10. *b.* $11,636
    Depreciable basis ÷ 27.5 years = annual depreciation
    $395,000 sale price – $75,000 land = $320,000 depreciable basis
    $320,000 ÷ 27.5 = $11,636 depreciable basis

11. *a.* 51.2%
    Operating expenses – reserves + annual mortgage payment ÷ PGI = cash break-even ratio
    $24,365 operating expenses – $10,000 reserves + $29,829 annual mortgage payment ÷ $86,400 PGI = .5115 or 51.2% cash break-even ratio

12. *b.* .1439 or .14
    NOI ÷ value = cap rate
    $56,851 NOI ÷ $395,000 sale price = .1439 or .14 cap rate

13. *a.* $865 debit seller; $865 credit buyer
    January (31) + February (28) + March (14) = 73 seller days
    $4,325 property taxes ÷ 365 = $11.8493 per day
    $11.8493 × 73 days of seller ownership = $865 debit seller; $865 credit buyer

14. *c.* $1,645.16 debit seller; $1,645.16 credit buyer
    $1,500 rent × 2 units = $3,000 total monthly rent
    31 days in month – 14 seller days = 17 days due buyer
    $3,000 ÷ 31 days = $96.7742 average rent per day
    $96.7742 × 17 days = $1,645.16 debit seller; $1,645.16 credit buyer

15. *a.* $326.74 debit seller; $326.74 credit buyer
    $723.50 interest in arrears ÷ 31 days = $23.3387 per day
    $23.3387 × 14 seller days = $326.74 debit seller; $326.74 credit buyer

16. *b.* $1,004.50; debit seller
    $143,500 sale price ÷ $100 = 1,435 taxable increments
    1,435 × $.70 = $1,004.50 doc stamps on deed; debit seller

17. *d.* $401.45; debit buyer
    $89,700 ÷ $100 = 897 taxable increments
    897 × $.35 = $313.95 doc stamps on assumed mortgage
    $25,000 ÷ $100 = 250 taxable increments
    250 × $.35 = $87.50 doc stamps on new mortgage
    $313.95 + $87.50 = $401.45 total doc stamps on note; debit buyer

18. *a.* $50; debit buyer
    $25,000 new mortgage × .002 = $50 intangible tax; debit buyer

19. *b.* $18,800
$143,500 sale price – $89,700 assumed mortgage
– $25,000 second mortgage =
$28,800 total down payment
$28,800 – $10,000 earnest money =
$18,800 additional down payment

20. *d.* $8,610 debit seller
$143,500 sale price × .06 = $8,610 debit seller

Index

A

Accrued depreciation
    definition of, 99, 101
    formula, 102, 103
    as percent, 104–5
    T-device, 104–5
Acre
    calculation of, 49, 52
    cost, 57–58
    square foot conversion to, 51
Actual age, 99, 102
Addition
    decimals, 17–18
    fractions, 14
Ad valorem tax, 87
Age-life method, 102–3
Amortization, 82–83
Amortized mortgage, 63, 79–81
Annual depreciation, 102
Area
    definition of, 43
    measure, 44
    multi-step problems, 58–59
    solving for, 53–54
    triangles, 54–56
Arithmetic
    basic concepts, 2–5
    operations, 10
Arrears, 131, 132
Assessed valuation, 87
Assumption of mortgage, 63, 76

B

Base (total)
    definition of, 29, 43
    formula for, 31, 33
    graduated commission calculation, 38–39
    multi-step calculation, 37
    T-device, 31–36
Before-tax cash flow, 122–23
Binder deposit, 142
Block, 44
Broker's statement, 143, 145

C

Calculator
    decimals, 18–21
    division of two numbers, 32
Cancelling, 15, 16
Capitalization rate, 99, 111, 112
Cash break-even ratio, 124
Cash flow, 122–23
Cash-on-cash return, 123
Cash throw-off, 122–23
Certificate of eligibility, 68
Closing statement
    parts of, 143
    preparation of, 141–43
    problems, 140–41
    seller's statement, 145
    work organizer for, 144–45
Commission
    calculation, 30
    graduated, 38–39
    net, 40–41
Common denominators, 12–14
Common factor, 12
Common fraction, 3, 9, 11
Comparable
    adjustments to, 108–9
    definition of, 99, 108
Conventional mortgage, 67–69, 74–75
Cost approach
    depreciation, 101–8
    explanation of, 100–1
    property value formula, 102
    reproduction cost new, 101
Cost per unit, 57–58
Credit
    closing statement, 142–43
    definition of, 129
    prorations, 130
Cubic measure, 57
Current value, remaining, 105–6

D

Debit
    closing statement, 142–43
    definition of, 129

    prorations, 130
    ratios, 74–75
    service, 122–23
Debt service coverage ratio (DSCR), 123–24
Decimal
    addition, 113–14
    conversions, 20–24, 30
    definition of, 1, 2
    division, 19–20
    multiplication, 18–19
    subtraction, 17–18
Decimal fraction
    definition of, 1, 3
    explanation of, 3–4
    rounding of, 5
Decimal point
    definition of, 1
    explanation of, 2
Decimal system
    definition of, 1
    explanation of, 2
Denominator
    definition of, 9, 11
    finding common, 12–14
Depreciable basis, 118
Depreciation
    age-life method, 102–3
    allowance, 117–18
    annual rate of, 105–6
    cost approach estimation, 101–8
    definition of, 99, 100
    formulas, 102, 103
    as percent, 103–6
    straight-line method, 101–2, 103–4, 118
    types of, 100–1
Digit
    definition of, 1
    explanation of, 2
    place value of, 2–4
Directional notation, 44
Direction indicators, 45–46
Discount points, 71–74
Dividend, 9, 19
Division
    decimals, 19–20
    fractions, 16–17

Divisor, 9, 16
Documentary stamp tax, 63, 75–77, 95–97, 142
Down payment
    conventional mortgage, 67–68
    FHA program, 69–71
DSCR. *See* Debt service coverage ratio

E

Economic life
    definition of, 99, 101–2
    T-device, 104
Effective age, 99
Effective gross income (EGI)
    definition of, 99, 112, 121
    formula, 121
    solving for, 113, 122
EGI. *See* Effective gross income
Equity dividend rate, 123
Expense section, closing statement, 143

F

Factor-of-23 method, 51
FHA Down Payment Simplification Act of 2002, 69
FHA 203(b) program, 69–71, 74–75
Financial investment analysis, 117–18
Fixed expense, 114
Formula
    accrued depreciation, 102
    age-life accrued depreciation, 103
    annual depreciation, 102
    annual depreciation allowance, 118
    area, 53, 54
    available loan, 68
    before-tax cash flow, 123
    capitalization rate, 112
    cash break-even ratio, 124
    cost approach, 100, 102
    debt service coverage ratio, 124
    down payment, 67
    effective gross income, 121
    equity dividend rate, 123
    gross income multiplier, 116
    housing expense ratio, 74
    income approach, 111
    interest, 64
    interest proration, 139
    loan-to-value ratio, 78
    net operating income, 111, 113, 122
    operating expense ratio, 124
    property tax proration, 135
    property tax revenue needed, 92, 93
    rent proration, 137
    taxable value, 88, 89

taxes owned, 89
tax savings, 90
30-day-month method, 131
360-day-statutory-year method, 132
365-day-year alternative method, 133
365-day-year method, 132
total obligations ratio, 74
total taxable value, 92, 93
volume, 57
Fraction
    addition, 14
    changing, 11–12
    conversions, 20–24, 30
    definition of, 9, 11
    division, 16–17
    explanation of, 11
    multiply, 15–16
    reducing, 12
    simplest form, 12, 14
    subtraction, 14
Frontage, 27
Functional utility, 100
Funding fee, 69

G

GIM. *See* Gross income multiplier
Government survey system, 43, 47–49
Graduated commission, 38–39
GRM. *See* Gross rent multiplier
Gross income multiplier (GIM), 115–17
Gross rent multiplier (GRM), 115–17

H

Height, 43
Homestead exemption, 87, 88
Housing expense ratio, 74

I

I. *See* Interest
Improper fraction, 9, 11
Income capitalization approach
    explanation of, 111–15
    formula, 111
    T-device, 111, 114
Index lease, 120–21
Information section, of closing statement, 143
Intangible tax, 63, 75
Interest (I)
    amortization, 80
    calculation of, 64–65
    definition of, 63
    proration, 139–40
    rate adjustment factor, 72
    in T-device, 65–66

Investment
    analysis, 117–18, 121–23
    economic ratios, 123–25
    future return, 123–25
    income tax problems, 118–19
    income types, 121–22
    index lease, 119–21
    percentage leases, 119–21

L

Land value, 101
Legal description
    government survey system, 47–49
    lot and block method, 44
    metes-and-bounds method, 45–47
Level-payment plan, 79
Linear measure, 44
Loan constants, 81
Loan-to-value ratio (LTV), 78
Lot, 44
Lot and block method, 43, 44
Lowest common denominator, 12–14
LTV. *See* Loan-to-value ratio

M

Market value, 99, 100
Maximum entitlement, 68–69
Measurements, 44
Memory device, 31–36. *See also* T-device
Metes-and-bounds, 43, 45–47
Mill, 87, 88
Millage rate, 92–93
Mixed number
    changing fractions, 11–12
    definition of, 1, 3, 9
Monuments, 45
Mortgage
    advanced problems, 79
    amortization, 79–81
    assumption of, 76
    balance, 72
    constant, 81
    debt ratios, 74–75
    definition of, 63
    discount points, 71–74
    financial packages, 67–71
    formulas, 64
    interest proration, 139–40
    payments, 77–78
    transfer tax, 75–77
Multiplication
    decimals, 18–19
    fractions, 15–16

N

National Housing Act, 69
Net commission, 40–41
Net operating income (NOI)
    before-tax cash flow, 122–23
    definition of, 99, 111, 112, 121
    economic ratios, 123–25
    formula, 111, 113, 122
    solving for, 113–14
NOI. *See* Net operating income
Numbers, 2
Numerator, 9, 11

O

Operating expense, 113–14
Operating expense ratio, 124

P–Q

P. *See* Principal
Parentheses, 12
Part
    formula for, 33
    graduated commission calculation, 38–39
    multi-step calculation, 37
    net commission calculation, 40–41
Percent
    conversions, 22–24, 30
    definition of, 9, 21, 29
    explanation of, 30, 31
    formula for, 31
    multi-step calculations, 37
    profit, 24–25
    solving for, 35–36
    symbol, 21
    T-device, 31–36
    variables, 31
    in word problems, 24–27
Percentage
    definition of, 29
    explanation of, 31
    formula for, 31
    T-device, 31–35
Percentage lease, 119–21
Per front foot, 43, 53
Perimeter, 43, 54
PGI. *See* Potential gross income
PITI. *See* Principal, interest, property taxes, and insurance
Place value
    conversion, 21
    definition of, 1
    explanation of, 2–4
PMI. *See* Private mortgage insurance
POB. *See* Point of beginning

Point of beginning (POB), 43, 45–46
Potential gross income (PGI)
    cash break-even ratio, 124
    definition of, 99, 112, 121
    solving for, 113, 122
Principal (P)
    definition of, 63
    new balance, 80
    reduction, 80
    in T-device, 65–66
Principal, interest, property taxes, and insurance (PITI), 74, 77–78
Private mortgage insurance (PMI), 67
Product, 9
Profit, 24
Proper fraction, 9, 11
Property tax
    city/county, 89–90
    exemptions, 90–91
    proration, 135–37
    special assessments, 94
    T-device use, 91–92
Prorate/proration
    closing statement, 142, 143
    definition of, 129, 130
    explanation of, 130
    mortgage interest, 139–40
    property tax, 135–37
    rent, 137–38
    30-day-month method, 131
    360-day-statutory-year method, 131–32
    365-day-year method, 132–34
Purchase price, 142
Quotient, 9, 16

R

R. *See* Rate of Interest
Rate
    definition of, 29, 30
    formula for, 31, 33
    graduated commission calculation, 38–39
    multi-step calculation, 37
    net commission calculation, 40–41
    T-device, 31–36
Rate of Interest (R)
    definition of, 63
    T-device, 65–66
Real property, transfer tax, 94–97
Rectangular survey system, 47–49
Rent, 137–38
Replacement cost new, 99, 100
Reproduction cost new, 99, 100, 101
Reserve for replacements, 114
Result (part)
    definition of, 29

formula for, 31
    T-device, 31–36
Rounding, 1, 4
Rounding place, 1, 4–5

S

Sales comparison approach, 108–11
Section, 47–49
Selling price, cost relationship, 25–26
Site value, 110–11
Special assessments, 87, 94
Square foot
    conversion to acres, 51
    cost per, 57–58
    multi-step problems, 52–53
Straight-line method, 101–4, 117–18
Subject property, 99, 108
Subtraction
    decimals, 17–18
    fractions, 14
Summation section, closing statement, 143
Symbols, 10

T

T. *See* Time
Taxable value
    definition of, 87
    explanation of, 88
    property tax and, 89–90
Tax rate, 88–89
    30-day-month method, 131
    360-day-statutory-year method, 131–32
    365-day-year method, 132–34
T-device, 31–36
    accrued depreciation, 104–5
    cost approach, 103–6
    income capitalization approach, 111, 114
    property tax, 91–92
    remaining current value, 105–6
    time in, 65–66
Time (T), 63, 65–66
Title closing, 129
Total
    formula for, 33
    net commission calculation, 40–41
Total obligation ratio, 74
Township, 47
Transfer tax, 75–77, 94–97
Triangle, 53–56

U

Useful life, 104
User's fee, 69

V

Vacancy and collection, 99
VA loan, 68–69, 74–75
Value
   adjustments to, 108–9
   cost approach, 100–8
   income capitalization approach, 111–15
   sales comparison approach, 108–11
   scale, 3

Variable expense, 114
Variable lease, 120–21
Volume
   definition of, 43
   formulas, 57
   measure, 44
   solving for, 53–54

W

Whole number
   changing fractions, 11–12
   definition of, 1, 3
   rounding of, 4, 5